The Practical Guide to the Apple //c

**by Peter C. Weiglin
and Joyce Conklin**

Addison-Wesley Publishing Company
Reading, Massachusetts • Menlo Park, California
London • Amsterdam • Don Mills, Ontario • Sydney

This book was printed from camera-ready mechanicals supplied by the authors.
Design by Mark J. Eaton

The words "Apple," "Lisa," and "Macintosh" as applied to computers are trademarks of Apple Computer, Inc.

VisiCalc is a trademark of Software Arts, Inc.

IBM is a registered trademark of International Business Machines, Inc.

BASIC is a trademark of the Dartmouth Board of Trustees.

Photographs courtesy of Apple Computer, Inc., and *Apple Orchard* Magazine.

ISBN 0-201-09660-9

ABCDEFGHIJ-HA-87654
First printing, May 1984

This volume is dedicated to:

Yoda

Moby

Sherri

Joy

Elf

Phido

Zelda

Chels

Lolly

Teri

Phillie

Jason

Teddy

. . . and to a very modest Mike Markkula.

Foreword

The Apple //c was introduced to the world on April 24, 1984. At the introduction ceremony, Apple President John Sculley stated that one of Apple's goals was to "change the ground rules for personal computer marketing."

Only time will determine the extent of Apple Computer's success in that endeavor. The feeling exists, however, that the Apple //c may in fact be the first *really* personal computer on the market. It is simple, it is portable, and it is compatible with the largest software library enjoyed by any personal computer. It has the characteristics that will endear it to people who have no intention (at least, no present intention) to become computer enthusiasts. Orders for well over 50,000 units were booked on the first day, which compares favorably even with Apple's Macintosh phenomenon.

In addition to the hardware, we have been impressed by the extent and quality of documentation and tutorials packed right in the box with each //c. This book, therefore, does not merely rehash the manuals, but seeks to provide additional information and insights to augment the material provided by the computer manufacturer.

Many people have assisted us in this effort. At Apple Computer, Lee Collings, Joseph Budge, and the Renees Olsen and Rodrique are individually acknowledged, but they are only the leaders of a much larger group. Mark J. Eaton and Nicole Lefcourt-Bolt of the *Apple Orchard* staff were indispensible. Addison-Wesley thoughtfully provided Amanda Hixson and Alan Goldstein to help steer us to publication. Jerry Martin fought valiantly to protect the integrity of the English language. Jeanne Weiglin allowed half of her house to be swallowed for the project and Joanne Short ferried documents; both women accompanied their aid with many helpful suggestions.

All of these people and many more deserve their share of whatever credit you may feel is due; the authors alone shoulder the responsibility for any errors. Our mutual goal is to help you to get the greatest possible satisfaction from your Apple //c.

Peter C. Weiglin

Joyce Conklin

San Mateo, CA April 1984

Contents

1

Your Own Computer?

The Amplified Mind

Most of history's significant technological developments have been amplifiers of human capability. They allow us to do more things faster and better than we could without them. Most of these developments improved our mobility: boats, railroads, automobiles, and airplanes. Another group of significant inventions, including numbers, language, and moveable type, increased people's ability to deal with information and to communicate.

The computer primarily improves or amplifies the *mind*, by enabling people to process more information at a faster rate. Note please that regardless of the science fiction writers, computers do not have minds of their own. It is, and always has been, people who do an amazing variety of things using computers as tools.

The Apple //c (say "two see") portable computer is the most powerful microcomputer of its size available today. There are smaller computers, and there are more powerful computers, but no combination of size and power equals the //c in the mid-1980s. Twenty-five years ago, the mind-amplifying power found in the //c would have cost more than a million dollars, and the machine itself would have filled a good-size room. Today, this computing power costs less than $1300 and the hardware fits into a briefcase. Further, you do not have to know how to program (create instructions for) a computer to use the //c, although the machine's built-in capabilities are extensive enough to provide a rewarding challenge for a long time if you want to learn. In fact, the Apple //c is an ideal machine on which to learn programming. You won't soon outgrow its power to help you learn.

Various experts have written volumes on the impact of placing the power of microcomputers in the hands of millions of individuals, so we'll spare you such philosophical musings here. The fact that you're reading this book shows that you're interested in expanding your individual information-processing capabilities. The Apple //c is an ideal way to do so, even if you don't know anything about computers right now.

Yesterday's "Gee Whiz"

The *idea* of automatic computers goes back to 1812 when Professor Charles Babbage of Cambridge University set out to build what he called a "difference engine" for math computations. The machine remained unbuilt after decades of work because in those days the components could not be fabricated with sufficient precision. In the 20th Century, Babbage's ideas took shape in the form of mechanical calculating machines, but even these were not automatic devices. In the 1930s, radio's vacuum tube electronics began to supplant mechanical devices in calculators. The vacuum tube was a "valve" with which one electric signal could control the power of another electrical signal. Developments such as this set the stage for the electronic computer, with the Bell Telephone Laboratories and other commercial and government groups seeking to develop ever-more powerful calculators.

If you were born after World War II, you're younger

than the first digital electronic computer. It was during that conflict that Britain's *Colossus I* and the U. S. Army's *ENIAC* ("Electronic Numerical Integrator And Calculator") began operation. These machines were used for such diverse purposes as helping to crack enemy codes and performing math calculations. Large arrays of vacuum tubes in metal frames were used in those machines. To the novice such steel-and-wire structures looked quite impressive. The large machines responsible for yesterday's "Gee whiz!" would be today's "Ho hum!" because the power of those room-filling giants was roughly equivalent to today's sophisticated pocket calculators.

The racks or frames of tubes ("mainframes" and peripheral frames) grew in power and size. Then, in 1948, the transistor was introduced by Bell Telephone Laboratories (now AT&T Technologies). Transistors perform the same kind of "valve" control function that vacuum tubes did, but they require much less power and space. Although computers continued to grow in power, they shrank in size and unit cost. Today, large numbers of transistors and other elements are grouped on single silicon chips about the size of a fingernail; these are called integrated circuits. Integrated circuits reduce the size and increase the power of computer components even more than transistors.

Integrated circuits were first used on mainframes to create increasingly complex mainframe computers. Then came the *mini*computers, which had the power of older mainframes, but occupied less space and cost less. Further development led to *micro*computers, of which the Apple //c is a new version.

The Portable Computer

Not too many years ago, a broadcast tape recorder weighing upwards of 50 pounds was called a "portable," chiefly because the manufacturer had thoughtfully provided (reinforced) handles. In those days, less than twenty years ago, today's broadcast-quality cassette recorders were a fond dream. So it is with computers. More than one computer manufacturer has attached a (reinforced) handle to a unit weighing 30 pounds or more. This indicates clearly that portability is in the eye of the manufacturer.

As the miniaturization of electronic circuitry evolves, however, computers are indeed becoming smaller. Some manufacturers of portable computers have included small black-and-white TV screen monitors and one or more magnetic storage devices called floppy disk drives. Some computers even contain a small printer within their sewing machine-size cases. A recent development is the use of a liquid crystal display (LCD) screen, like that seen on many digital watches, in place of the bulky TV monitor. With LCD display screens, computers can become even more portable.

The Apple //c is also a "portable" computer; it weighs only seven and a half pounds, and it has a handle. One of the reasons the computer's main unit ("central processing unit", or "CPU") weighs so little is because its power supply is a separate unit. The power supply is small enough not to require a handle. Built into the CPU case is a 5-1/4-inch disk drive.

While the //c does not contain the video screen in its own case, the machine is designed to accommodate a number of video display devices. Because the //c has built-in display capability for color as well as monochrome (that's another name for black-and-white), the variety of possible video display units that might be attached to it is large enough that a single built-in unit wouldn't really satisfy anybody. Apple is offering a 9-inch monochrome video monitor for the //c. A special flat-screen LCD display unit is targeted for late 1984 availability. If you prefer, color monitors or other larger monochrome monitors may be used, so you get to pick your video display. The //c becomes either the most portable or the least portable of computers, as you choose.

But What Does it Do?

Any computer, regardless of size, takes in information, processes that information in some way, and returns the processed information to you. A computer can use its electronic circuitry to add and subtract in the same way that calculators do. The computer can also be instructed to follow a complex sequence of pre-planned (or "programmed") steps. A computer program can instruct the computer to compare two items to see if they are the same or not, and then guide the computer's next actions by the result of that comparison. By themselves, these functions aren't spectacular; the computer achieves its amazing results by performing thousands of these simple operations each second.

Those are the basics. In terms of useful work, most people use computers for four functions: word processing, financial analysis (spreadsheets) and accounting, ordering of related information (data management), and simulation (largely games). These will be covered in detail in a later chapter. These functions are essentially the same regardless of the size or complexity of the computer involved; the only real difference is that bigger computers can handle more information in any one span of time.

Computers built during the Dark Ages (before 1975) required expert operators who spoke the computers' "languages". These experts became known as Data Processing (DP) Specialists. They acted as the buffer between the computer and the humans who needed the information that the computer could produce. It's no accident that these folks were referred to cynically as

"High Priests," and it should be no surprise that the DP folks took their roles very seriously. The psychological bias and assumption of most people was that computers and their human keepers existed to serve institutions, not individuals. The exceptions, of course, were those individuals who controlled the companies or agencies that owned the computers.

To some extent, it was good business for the makers and operators of computers to foster the high level of awe that characterized the general public's attitude toward these mainframe computers and the people who attended them. It meant, among other things, that fewer people dared to question the operators' salaries or computer purchase prices. In those days, the average person did not directly control the power of the computer.

When the microcomputer came upon the scene in 1975, that psychology began to change. Here was a machine that could be operated directly by the individual who needed the information. Going back to our amplification analogy for a moment, the microcomputer or personal computer is to the large mainframe computer as the private automobile is to the transit bus or trolley. In each case a similar function is performed. With either mainframes or personal computers it is the processing of data; with autos and buses it is moving from one place to another. But, with automobiles and personal computers you are no longer dependent on someone else to get something done. You now have freedom of choice. Before you can exercise your freedom, though, you need to learn to "drive" your own machine.

Hardware and Software   All computers achieve their results through a combination of hardware and software. Hardware isn't hard to figure out: it's the tubes, transistors, silicon chips, mountings, connections, and the other electronic and mechanical parts necessary for the machine to work. In the case of the Apple //c, you won't have to worry about the hardware (insides) because, unlike previous Apple models, the case is never opened in use.

Functionally, computer hardware contains input/output (I/O) circuitry to process data into and out of the machine, and a processing unit to manipulate the information. The computer also has a memory storage area (like the banks of boxes at the Post Office, each with its own address), and a control unit to oversee the operations of the other three units. All of these exist as tiny electrical circuits on various silicon chips inside the box.

While we have provided a glossary as a part of this book, let's stop here and cover two somewhat confusing hardware-related terms we often hear. These are "RAM" and "ROM". RAM stands for Random Access Memory which means that the information contained in this memory can be directly addressed, read, manipulated, expanded, deleted and changed in many ways during the computer's operation. When you turn off the computer, the information stored in RAM memory is erased and lost. ROM chips use "Read Only Memory". These chips store information permanently. You can't "write" information to them. Chips of this type are permanently programmed at the factory and can't be changed. In the Apple //c, there is "128K of RAM," which means that just over 128,000 characters can be stored and accessed in memory. Some of that memory will be used by data (such as your address list), and some memory will be taken up by the software.

"Software" is the name given to the sets of instructions that control or program your computer's sequence of activities. Note that while these programs most often are stored on a vinyl floppy disk, the disk is not the software; just as a phonograph record is not the music recorded on it.

What would you like your computer to be right now? A pinball machine? A word processor? A stock portfolio analyzer? A home security controller? A giant accounting spread sheet? A roster of your church's membership? A mathematics or spelling instructor for your child? The //c can be all of these things, and many more, depending on the "software" that you load into it to control the flow of electrons through its hardware.

Here's a brief example:

```
10   HOME
20   PRINT "Type Your Name and press <RETURN>:"
30   INPUT YN$
40   PRINT YN$
```

This is an example of a program written in in a programming "language" called BASIC (ridiculous acronym defined in the glossary). This program has four elements: First, HOME (a command) instructs the computer to clear the screen. Second, the computer is instructed to write the words, "Type Your Name and Press «RETURN»:" on the screen. Third, the computer receives the information (input) that you type. After you press the «RETURN» key, it stores that "string" of typed characters in memory and gives it a name, "YN$". Fourth, the computer fetches the string of characters it knows as "YN$" from memory and outputs (prints) it on the screen. That four-line sequence of instructions is a program. It is also software, just as much as the longest financial analysis program ever written is software.

With the Apple //c you're not limited to programs developed by others. You can in fact write your own programs for your own needs. The Apple //c is a small computer, but it is more powerful than other machines in similar-sized cases. Your $1300 has purchased a package equivalent to a system costing $3000 just two years ago. Clearly, the potential for improving the results of many personal activities is now available to a much larger group of people. We have come a long way since the days of the high priests.

Now the Bad News . . .

If the machine is given the right instructions by the human who controls it, the data will be received, processed and be returned as useful information. But here's the bad news: If it is given wrong instructions, it will follow those just as if they were correct. In short, the machine does what you tell it to do — which may not always be what you want it to do. The same computer that lets you do the equivalent of three days of paperwork in one hour will also allow you to make mistakes at an undreamed-of rate.

In other words, the microcomputer will not save us from our sins. If you have sloppy work habits, it will not make you neat. If you are a procrastinator, the computer will not enforce timeliness. It *will* help you to create, identify, and modify a schedule, and tell you exactly how far behind schedule you are — which you may or may not find comfortable. The computer can do all of these things with a schedule, but you'll still have to live up to the schedule you create. These facts, by the way, explain why the science fiction people are off-base in their characterizations of computers as "superbrains" that will dominate society because they lack human imperfections. The mind amplifier, under human control, also amplifies human imperfections, with stunningly high fidelity.

In the next chapter, we'll look at how a group of imperfect humans brought Apple computers into the world, and how they created the "plug-in" personal computer movement. We will also see how they started a revolution in the process.

You may know that your purchase of the Apple //c places you among those who benefit from the revolution.

What you may not know is that waiting until now has helped you to escape much of the tribulation of the Apple computer's growing pains. There was a time when there were no disk drives for the Apple. There was a time when an 80-column-wide Apple screen display with lower-case letters was a dream. There was a time when only the most rudimentary software was available, and it was not very user-friendly.

It has become fashionable to say that those growing pains were fun, but let's face it: many times, those of us with early Apple models weren't sure we could stand much more of this "fun". If you do remember those days, the //c can only be a source of wonder for you. Many people at Apple call the //c their company's "first real personal computer" because of its combination of small size and great power. Let's see how it came to be.

2

The //c's Heritage

Apple Seeds   Your Apple //c personal computer is part of an amazing growth process. If we were to draw the "family Apple tree," it would look like this:

Figure 2-1

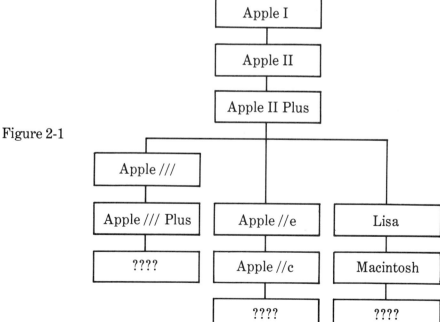

Steven Wozniak

The first Apple computer came into being because a young Hewlett-Packard engineer named Steven ("Woz") Wozniak wanted his own personal computer terminal. The year was 1975. In many companies and universities, networks of remote terminals were connected to mainframe computers. For those in selected offices, that was the very limited beginning of individual access to the power of a computer system.

At that time, many of us shared Woz's desire to have individual terminals, but we were in no position to do much about it. Woz, on the other hand, was able to marry his desire with his ability to build such a device. Using his abilities as an engineer, he built his own terminal and telephone modulator/demodulator (modem) which he used to connect his terminal to a mainframe computer via telephone lines.

Also in 1975, a handful of electronics hobbyists were beginning to build their own microcomputers. These folks formed the Homebrew Computer Club to share information on how to build and improve their rudimentary computers. So, beginning in 1975, the Homebrew Club, located in the San Francisco Bay area, provided the forum for the exchange of microcomputer ideas and improvements. It also spawned an array of small companies manufacturing kits based on the then-new microprocessor chips. Company names like MITS, Altair, SPHERE, IMSAI and Mark 8 became familiar to the aficionados.

While we consider their efforts primitive today, these individuals were then pushing the limits of computer technology as best they could. These pioneers had to overcome many obstacles, not the least of which was the cost of components. In those days, no large companies were backing their developments. Chips such as the popular Model 8080 microprocessor were priced at a hefty $270 each, a price that was clearly beyond the reach of most Homebrewers. Despite such hardships, members of the Homebrew Club, and others like it, continued to develop innovative hardware and software.

As Steve Wozniak tells it, he was amazed to hear one day in 1975 that a new microprocessor chip, called the Mostek model 6502, was being sold for only $20. *That* he could afford. Within a short time he bought one, and was buried in the manual on the bus ride home. Today, almost two million Apple computers, including your //c, contain variations of the 6502 microprocessor. The reason why is simple: Woz's one-man design team couldn't afford the "better" 8080 chip at the time.

By November 1975, Steve had built his bargain chip into a handmade circuit board. He had also discovered how to use the 6502's simpler internal operating characteristics to make it comparable to the more expensive chips. Woz also devised operating software to connect both a teletype keyboard and a TV set to the chip. In addition, he wrote (from scratch) a new version of the BASIC language, the dialect that became known as Integer BASIC. That first unit had 4,096 bytes (4K) of RAM memory, which was considered a significant achievement at the time. Today, your Apple //c has 128K of RAM, or 32 times as much.

Steven Jobs

Enter another hobbyist, Steven Jobs, who had some suggestions about memory and configurations. As the two Steves worked together and got to know each other, a new machine evolved. It was a small microcomputer that talked Wozniak's Integer BASIC. During this period, Hewlett-Packard actually turned down and released employee Wozniak's design; the large company wasn't interested. Other hobbyists saw and liked the design, and even asked for copies. It was Steve Jobs who asked the fateful question, "Why don't we form a company and sell a few PC boards?" Woz agreed.

The New Company

To fund the company, Woz sold his HP calculator ("they were coming out with a new model anyway"), and Jobs sold his Volkswagen van. With their new capital, they engaged a designer to lay out the wiring paths for the computer's printed circuit board and production was under way. The two entrepreneurs went off to the Santa Clara County Court House to register their new company. First question: What was the company's name to be? Dozens of names were considered, but all of the good ones appeared to have been taken. Jobs, munching on an apple, said in frustration, "If we can't think of a name by the time they close, let's call it 'Apple'." Closing time came without further brainstorms, and "Apple" it was; temporarily, they thought, until something better could be devised.

Shortly thereafter, the two Steves unleashed about 200 Apple I circuit boards on an unsuspecting world. The year was 1976. The original Apple computer was really only a printed circuit board. Buyers had to buy or scrounge a separate power supply, video monitor, and keyboard. These three items were not supplied by Apple, but were available through surplus shops. The most important thing about the Apple I was that it worked, and with a little effort it could be used to store data on an ordinary audio cassette tape recorder.

The Apple II Revolution

The two entrepreneurs continued to make improvements. Wozniak decided to equip the machine for color video displays, and he and Jobs found a way to put the keyboard and circuitry in one case. The result was the Apple II, a microcomputer with its operating system and Woz's Integer BASIC in ROM storage. The original 4K of RAM memory was there, but now the computer could be expanded to an amazing 48K. This all fit into a simple box with a new, built-in keyboard. There also were eight slots for plugging in smaller circuit boards to further expand the Apple II's capabilities. They felt that with luck they could be producing fifty computers a month; some people thought the entrepreneurs were too optimistic.

Steve and Steve had a real product, but in order to bring the Apple II to market, they needed both financing and organization — which they didn't have. The answer came to Apple in the person of A. C. ("Mike") Markkula, who dropped into the firm's garage headquarters one day. Already successful and semi-retired, despite being only in his early thirties, Markkula nurtured the dream of building a company quickly enough for it to become one of the 500 largest American companies within five years. Impressed by what he saw on Wozniak's

The Classic Apple II system

workbench, Markkula developed a plan and arranged the venture capital financing for that dream. While Markkula has remained somewhat in the background, those who joined the company in its first year claim that his part in Apple's success was equal to that of the two better-known founders.

There were other small computers on the market by 1977, but none did what the Apple II could do, despite its "bargain" 6502 processor chip. One feature that set the Apple II apart was that it had color capabilities by 1977. More importantly, a number of other small companies was sprouting up to supply not only software, but additional hardware for the Apple II. Small circuit boards for special functions were designed and sold to fit into the eight slots Woz thoughtfully provided in the Apple's "motherboard," or main circuit board. This kind of Apple-specific support made the II even more appealing to consumers, and put Apple way ahead of its competition.

The Apple II was an "open architecture" system, one in which the information about how the system works is available to the user, rather than being hidden and confidential. That approach was new and different, given the then-prevailing psychology of computer hardware designers. Computers prior to the Apple were mysterious objects. Manufacturers doled out as little information as possible about the inner workings of their machines. Apple actually released detailed system information, and even included better-than-average user manuals, another step in promoting better understanding of their machines.

That information flow, and the encouragement it gave to others who would manufacture Apple-related products, proved to be a major factor in Apple's success. Another factor was the network of user groups that grew up around the Apple, a phenomenon covered more thoroughly in Chapter 9 of this book.

Apple Computer, Inc. moved out of the garage to offices in Cupertino, California in 1977. From their original 1200-square-foot office space the company began expanding until they occupied more than ten nearby buildings. As sales of the Apple II continued to grow, the company added more facilities in other states and countries. Over the next two years, an estimated 50,000 Apple II computers were shipped from Cupertino, and Mike Markkula put the company's infrastructure into place. By 1979, Apple was poised for significant market gains, ones that exceeded everyone's expectations.

Sales grew from $47.8 million in 1979 to $982.8 million in 1983. This growth was largely due to a revised machine, called the Apple II Plus. The new model was essentially an Apple II, but the ROMs were changed to include an improved version of BASIC called Applesoft, which was used in place of the original Integer BASIC. (Note: some users have claimed that Applesoft was not an improvement over Integer, a claim which is reminiscent of arguments over the merits of the stick shift vs. the automatic transmission. The argument is immaterial anyway, since Applesoft is now by far the more widely-used language and is the form of the BASIC language resident in your //c.) While official figures were never released, unofficial estimates place the number of Apple IIs and II Pluses produced at about 800,000 worldwide.

A Good Machine Done Wrong

In 1980, Apple Computer made a mistake. The company introduced a new, more powerful computer, which they named the Apple /// (Three). While the Apple /// was another innovative step in microcomputer architecture, the machine suffered dismal sales and bad press because it was rushed to market before it was fully tested. Horror stories began to circulate about failures and frustrations faced by early purchasers of the machine.

The Apple ///

Most of the problems related to poor component quality or manufacturing practices, not to the computer's design. The beleagured Apple folks worked strenuously to correct the problems, but the Apple /// got a reputation as a "dog," a machine that was no darn good.

An example: an Apple ///, in use, would stop working. Just stop. Dead. The owner took it back to the dealer, who plugged it in and started it up. Worked fine. The owner took it home. Thirty minutes later, the Apple /// would die again. It turned out that the chips were not making proper contact with their sockets. That's an error that would have been discovered if the sockets had been tested properly. The "fix?" Drop the machine from a height of four to six inches onto a tabletop. This jarring motion reseated the chips. It was the hi-tech version of kicking the vending machine.

After solving the problems, and replacing an estimated 4,000 of its early machines at no charge to the
owners, Apple has sold almost 100,000 Apple ///s. Most
Apple /// users would not give up their machines
without a fight, but Apple learned a valuable lesson from
the Apple ///: Rushing to introduce a model that really
hasn't been fully tested gives your company a black eye.

Changing Markets

By 1981, microcomputers were no longer the toys of
computer hobbyists. More and more of the machines
were being purchased by people with little interest in the
computer itself; consumers began to see computers as
tools for getting some kind of work done. For many of
these buyers, the Apple II was not the best product. It
required additional hardware to produce a screen display with 80 columns of information. The SHIFT key on
the keyboard did not work properly without modification, and lower-case letters were not available unless you
hae the required extra hardware. Human nature being
what it is, attention was now being focused on the Apple
II's "shortcomings" in the changing market place.

IBM, by far the largest company in the computer field,
awakened to the potential of the microcomputer market
at this time. Apple's misstep with the ///and the Apple
II's limitations presented IBM with the perfect opportunity to enter the market. In Fall 1981, IBM introduced
its Personal Computer, or "PC," selling it as a machine
that had none of the Apple "problems." With the PC,
IBM was successful in capturing an increasing share of
the market from Apple. Another reason for IBM's success was their focus on selling to business customers
who were unfamiliar with microcomputers but were
familiar with the IBM name on mainframe computers.

The IBM PC uses a model 8088 microprocessor chip
and an operating system that is not directly compatible
with your Apple //c. Several other manufacturers have

introduced computers that are compatible with the PC, and there is also a 30-pound "portable" or two in that group. Much of the software on the market is now issued in two versions, one for the Apple and one for the IBM. The fact that manufacturers include both versions illustrates Apple's strength in the market.

The Other Apple Family

In January 1983, Apple introduced two new computer models, the Lisa and the Apple //e. The Lisa is Apple's largest computer model, and it does not use the 6502 microprocessor. Instead, the Lisa contains the 32-bit Motorola Model 68000 microprocessor. Lisa was the first member of Apple's "68000 family" of computers. The

Apple's Lisa; Model 2/10 shown.

Apple //e and ///, and the Apple //c, are members of the longer-established "6502" chip family.

The 68000 family was the result of more than two years of work by Apple in their attempts to build a computer that would make software easier to use. It's development was one of the few instances in which a software engineer, John Couch, headed a hardware design project. The project was top secret, and was code-named "Lisa," after a female in the life of a design team member. Apple was using female code names for its projects during that period. The ///, for example, was said to have been called "Diana," and the Apple //c answered to "Lolly," "Teri," and other names for a while. (Was it equal rights that prompted the "Jason" code name for the //c later on?)

Like the Apple II, the Lisa was a breakthrough. On this machine, "programs" per se were not the user's concern. More than one project could be viewed on the screen's "electronic desktop" at the same time. A small rolling box called a mouse was the primary control device for the computer. What really set the Lisa apart was that enough could be learned about it in twenty minutes to begin using it. Until then, the average, basic-entry learning time had been about four hours. Apple sprung a small surprise. The machine was introduced under what had been its preproduction code name, "Lisa," which was now solemnly declared to stand for "Local Integrated Software Architecture." An industry pundit suggested that a more appropriate name might be, "Let's Invent Some Acronym."

A product related to the Lisa technology, code-named "Macintosh," was also under development at that time. Introduced in January 1984, the Macintosh computer turned out to be Lisa's younger sibling in the 68000 chip family. Lisa and Macintosh are technically similar, and can run some of the same software. They are not directly

compatible with the Apple //c. The Lisa and Macintosh projects were carried on separately from the Apple II and /// "6502 family" of computers.

The Apple //e

Meanwhile, another set of Apple engineers was wrestling with Apple II improvements and trying to make it easier to manufacture. Remember, the original production target had been 50 units per month, and the combined production rate of Apple's factories in 1981 was about 400 times that. The first such improved model, announced on the same day as Lisa, was the Apple //e ("e" for "enhanced," they tell us). The //e's design improved on many of the Apple II and II Plus features. It integrates the installation of a card for 80-column dis-

The Apple //e

play and 128K of RAM memory. The //e uses a standard typewriter keyboard layout rather than the Apple II's teletype-based keyboard. (It's interesting to note that IBM, having created the standard keyboard with its Selectric typewriter, abandoned it for the PC, while Apple adopted the familiar layout for the //e.) The Apple //e design improvements created a more people-oriented computer. The manufacturing improvements created a lower-cost computer.

What frequently happens during redesign of a product is that the software for the new model will not work with the older model. The //e designers and marketers were convinced that they should not let this happen. Rather than abandon the Apple II users, Apple tested and retested existing Apple II software to make sure that as many of its programs as possible could run on the new machine.

The Apple //e has been even more successful than the II Plus. According to unofficial sources, almost as many //es were sold during its first year as Apple II Pluses in four years. The widest variety of software available for any computer belongs to the Apple // family.

The Apple //c, introduced in Spring 1984, represents a further improvement over the Apple //e. It uses the latest version of the 6502 processor chip, the 65C02. The //c also includes internal circuitry for interfacing with disks, printers, and other peripherals without the need for plug-in auxilliary cards. In short, the Apple //c is ideal for the serious computer user as well as the hobbyist. Now that we've seen how it came to be, let's take a look at the machine itself.

The //c's
electronic innards

The contents of the
Apple //c Box

3

Introducing the //c

The Apple //c is physically the smallest member of the Apple "6502 family" of microcomputers, but it is by no means the least powerful. Its standard RAM memory configuration is 128K. Billed as a portable computer, the //c weighs only 7.5 lbs. (3.4 kg.). Unlike other Apple // models, the //c has a built-in disk drive accessible from its right side. The //c contains circuitry for many functions and interfaces that required additional costly hardware on the II Plus and //e models (and which still require extra-cost "optional" hardware on other brands of computers).

The //c has none of the internal expansion slots that characterized the older microcomputers in the Apple // family. On the II Plus and //e, eight of these slots are used for (1) adding printer interfaces (usually in Slot 1), (2) expanding RAM memory (in Slot 0 of the II Plus or in the special auxilliary slot of the //e), (3) connecting a communications modem (usually Slot 2 or 4), (4) adding the controller card for external disk drives (Slot 6), and (5) inserting cards to generate an 80-column-wide display (Slot 3 on the II Plus, or the auxilliary slot on the //e). Expansion slots were also used to add many other boards such as clock cards for constant timing functions, extra ROM boards with machine language programs built in, and much more.

The marketing of add-on boards for the II Plus and //e was, and still is, a thriving adjunct industry, providing many companies with continuing revenues. Some of the companies that supply add-on boards of this type are descendants of those started by Homebrew Club members. These companies survive, in part, because specialized functions such as synthesized music or process -control applications can currently only be accommodated by the addition of plug-in cards. Because the //c lacks expansion slots, you'd have to get an Apple //e, an Apple /// (or a used II Plus) if you wanted to accomplish tasks of this sort. But, as you'll see, the lack of expansion slots does not mean that the //c is a limited or "stripped-down" microcomputer.

The //c has the full upper- and lower-case text display ability that is standard on the //e, and the //c has 128K of user-accessible memory (RAM). It also has built-in 40- and 80-column display capability (mentioned above), a built-in disk drive (no cable needed) with control circuitry, and a serial port (socket) for the printer connection. Further, there is a second serial port for a modem or other peripheral device, a port for the attachment of game paddles, joystick or mouse, and a port used to attach a second disk drive. The standard //c is comparable to an Apple //e with its auxilliary slot and three (or four) other slots already filled with add-on boards.

Portability

Just because it has a handle, is it portable? Most "portable" computer models are perhaps better called "transportables." They have handles, can be grunted under an airplane seat, and must have 110-volt AC transformers to operate. But, the //c is more versatile and hence more portable (more on this in a moment).

There is no built-in display screen in the //c, so the display unit must be carried as a separate box. Two different screens are being manufactured by Apple specifically for the //c: a nine-inch monitor, and a flat-screen LCD display unit (introduction date late 1984).

*The 9-inch Apple //c
Monitor*

The flat-screen unit plugs into the back of the //c and can display the standard 24-line by 80-character screen display. The //c computer, with its power supply, flat-screen display unit, and the necessary software and manuals, will fit into most "standard" briefcases. (Note that while there is really no standard for briefcase size,

The Flat-Panel Display

(each briefcase manufacturer seems to know best), the //c carrying case *is* about the size of a briefcase. The second disk drive is not provided for in the //c carrying case, but we have fitted it into a briefcase along with the //c. The nine-inch screen monitor will not fit into a briefcase; the cathode ray tube video display remains the most difficult computer-system component to miniaturize.

So, the //c with either display version (nine-inch or flat screen) is portable, and could even be used outdoors. It would be a mistake to equate portability of any computer with ruggedness, however. The //c just is not as rugged as a camp stove. You should be aware that the //c will

operate best in the temperature range of 50 to 104
degrees Farenheit (10 to 40 degrees Centigrade), and
that it will operate best if it is not banged around. It will
operate poorly, or not at all, if liquids are spilled on it —
particularly if they're spilled into the keyboard.

Power Supply

There were some problems with the power supply
(transformer) in earlier Apple II models. It was barely
adequate to meet the power needs of the machine, let
alone one with a few added auxilliary cards installed.
And, since it was inside the computer's case, it
generated unwanted heat. To help eliminate some of the
heat problems (and to increase portability), the //c uses
a new kind of electronic chip that was not used in former
Apple II models. Called the "CMOS" type (which de-
scribes its internal construction process to the engineers), this chip consumes less electricity and generates
less heat. To further reduce heat problems, Apple
decided to place the //c power supply in a separate box,
about 2½" x 2¾" x 5¼", (6 x 7 x 13 cm.) and provided
ventilation openings in the main CPU to cool the computer even further. It's not a good idea to block or cover
these openings in the top or bottom of your machine. For
example, don't put the //c on a cushioned surface that
would block airflow. Heat buildup can cause electric
parts to do funny things.

One of the two cords attached to the power supply
plugs into a wall outlet. Make sure that you're using a
properly grounded three-wire outlet. Don't cheat by
using one of those two-wire circuit adapter plugs. The
seven-pin connector on the power supply's other cord
plugs into a socket on the //c. If you're looking at the
back of the //c, it's at the far right. There's only one socket that accommodates the seven-pin plug.

Once installed, the power supply provides 15-volt DC
power to the //c. This voltage is equivalent to that pro-

vided by the power supplies in many vehicles. What that means to you is that it is possible to run your //c by hooking it up to an automotive or battery power supply. If a 15-volt DC portable monitor or display is used, the //c can become truly "portable". You would not be limited to the length of a 110-volt AC cord. You'll be able to carry your //c to, and use it in, remote locations. We do not expect much time to elapse before the equipment that allows such portability is on the market. Your dealer should be able to help you set up such a system; unfortunately, the details of such a setup are beyond the scope of this book.

Disk Drives
The //c contains one built-in disk drive that uses 5-1/4-inch floppy diskettes. The unit is fully compatible with Apple's standard 35-track, 16-sector disk formats. The capacity of a disk is about 140,000 bytes of information, roughly equivalent to two-thirds of this book. The //c's disk-drive mechanism has a lower profile than the drives that plugged into Apple's earlier models, and is called a "half-high" drive. To save even more space, Apple engineers shrank the disk-drive control circuitry as well. In the Apple II Plus and //e (and in other personal computers) the disk-drive circuits are located on an auxilliary disk controller card plugged into one of the expansion slots. In the //c, that circuitry is located in one chip on the main circuit board, or "motherboard".

Apple makes a second disk drive that comes in its own "half-high" box. It is plugged into one of the sockets on the back of the //c. Note that the disk-drive cable connector plug is not the same as that used on older Apple models. The second //c disk drive uses a 19-pin "D-type" connector whose cable and internal connections are more rugged than those of the delicate ribbon cables used on the Apple II and //e. Unlike the larger Apple machines, no more than two disk drives can be used with the //c - - one built-in and one external. That's all.

The //c disk drives are designed to run most of the software that would run on the Apple //e and Apple II Plus computers. That's good, because these computers have the largest single catalog or "base" of software items available. Other language systems that operate on the //e (such as Pascal and Logo) will also operate on the //c.

Without testing all of the available software programs (an impossible task here), there's no reliable way to tell which programs will or will not work on a new machine. Even after a full round of testing, the results would be immediately out of date because software companies continually issue upgraded versions of popular programs. Another problem arises because some companies use different disk copy-protection schemes in an attempt (usually futile) to keep people from making copies of the disks. In fact, some companies use different protection schemes on different copies of the same product.

Some software, primarily games, will not operate on the //c. In most cases, this is because the software manufacturers used disk copy-protection schemes based on the different mechanical characteristics of older Apple disk drives. Also, programs that require the CP/M or MS-DOS operating systems will not operate on the //c because there are no CP/M or MS-DOS adapters for it.

The best way to determine if software is compatible with your computer is to check the package to see if it is clearly marked as compatible with the //c. If you see a compatibility notice or sticker, the manufacturer has done his homework. Even if you can't find a marking that indicates whether a particular II Plus or //e software product runs on the //c, you can still be reasonably sure that it will run because most leading companies' products are likely to be //c-compatible. As a final check, ask the dealer to try the program on a //c at the store before you buy.

Earlier in this chapter we mentioned the external second disk drive available for the //c. One reason a second drive is so important is that without one, you'll be swapping disks back and forth as you run your programs, and that can become a pain. Many software packages run much more easily if you use a two-drive system which has the program disk in Drive 1 and the disk with your data on it in Drive 2. Because of the frustration you will avoid by having a second drive, we recommend that you purchase one as soon as possible. Further, having only one drive complicates life when you make a backup copy of a disk. We'll discuss backups a bit later in this chapter.

Working with Disks

First things first: the door latch on a //c disk drive is a bit tricky until you get the hang of it. Generally, to open the door you push the latch in and up. Push down on the latch to close the door after inserting the disk. If you turn on the computer and there is no disk in the built-in drive, the screen will display a message asking you to check the disk drive. That's an improvement over the older Apple models, which would whirr forever if you forgot to insert your disk.

To access programs or data stored on a disk, you need to tell the computer which drive has the needed information. That's known as "calling" a drive. Apple has retained the conventional call for disk drives used on its older models. The primary disk drive called in an Apple system was usually connected to Drive Position 1 on a peripheral card plugged into Slot 6. The drive was called Slot 6, Drive 1, or "S6,D1". Even though there are no peripheral cards and no actual slots in the //c, the built-in drive is still addressed as Slot 6, Drive 1, just as it was on the older models. The one external disk drive permitted with the //c is known as Slot 6, Drive 2. This was done to keep the older software compatible with the //c. The standard keyboard commands PR#6 and IN#6 work without change.

Any computer with disk drives uses a Disk Operating System (DOS) to operate. The DOS is a program that acts as a "traffic cop" for the computer. When you start up a //c system with a system disk in the built-in drive, the first thing that happens is that an instruction from the operating system tells the computer to load the rest of the operating system into memory — somewhat like pulling yourself up by your own bootstraps. That's why we use the term "booting" to describe the process of turning on the machine. Your //c will work well with Apple ProDOS, DOS 3.3, Pascal, and other Apple language operating systems. It will not work with the CP/M or MS-DOS operating systems.

Under the DOS 3.3 and Pascal operating systems, only the internal disk drive can be used to start or "boot" the system. With ProDOS, either drive can be used. To boot from a ProDOS disk in the //c's external drive, the command is PR#7.

ProDOS

Apple's new disk operating system is called ProDOS. It came about because Apple Computer's DOS 3.3 operating system would not work well with their ProFile hard (rigid) disk. The ProFile five-megabyte hard disk drive has the storage capacity of 35 floppy disks, but DOS 3.3 can only treat hard disks like a group of floppies. There's no flexibility. So, hard disk manufacturers developed "patches," or modifications to the DOS 3.3 program, to accommodate their products. Unfortunately, each company did it differently. In response, Apple developed ProDOS.

ProDOS is adapted from the Sophisticated Operating System ("Apple SOS") introduced with and for the Apple /// in 1980. SOS and ProDOS are less dependent on having specific hardware present, and operate with a wider variety of devices. The ProDOS disk format is different from, and not compatible with, DOS 3.3. It is, however, compatible with SOS, which means that data files can be transported between Apple //c's, //e's, and ///'s.

Each "file" on a ProDOS disk has its own name. That file may be independent or it may be part of a "subdirectory" — a group of files. You identify a disk and file by its "pathname" (volume name plus subdirectory name(s) plus file name) rather than by calling the drive holding the disk. Each disk is a "volume." Think of it as an electronic loose-leaf binder in which you keep data files. Here's an example:

`/RAILROAD/FREIGHT/BOX.CARS`

would be a file listing the **BOX.CARS**, which is a sub-category of **FREIGHT** cars, on a disk volume for the **RAILROAD. /FREIGHT** is a subdirectory. A slash precedes each name, acting as a separator. It's like having a loose-leaf binder marked RAILROADS, in which an index tab marked FREIGHT marks a section containing the file, BOX CARS.

Note again that ProDOS focuses is on the disk volume, not on the hardware device (the drive) housing the volume. If you used DOS 3.3, you called for the hardware location, say "Slot 6, Drive 2." If the correct disk wasn't there, DOS 3.3 would have a nervous breakdown. With ProDOS, the disk volume named /RAILROAD in our example can be in either drive; ProDOS will look for and find it.

There's a bit less flexibility in file names with ProDOS than with DOS 3.3. ProDOS file names must start with a letter; and may contain only letters, numbers, and periods. Now you see why that file name example above ("**BOX.CARS**") has a period in it. Spaces can't be used, so you use the period to separate words. It helps your eye to recognize a file name.

Filenames can't be more than 15 characters long, and no complete pathname can exceed 64 characters. In practice, volume and subdirectory names are usually shortened, anyway. The example cited above easily shortens to:

   /RR/FRT/BOX.CARS

"Filer", which appears on the ProDOS User's Disk, includes the programs for copying files from one disk to another and for formatting blank disks. You must use the Filer program to format a blank disk before using it with the //c. The computer will ask you for the location of the disk-drive containing the blank disk, and for the name you want to give to the volume. If you don't specify a name, the Filer will call the volume "**/BLANK**" and assign it a number beteen 00 and 99. If you later think of a better name than "**/BLANK55**," you can use the Filer to rename a volume at any time.

The ProDOS Filer also contains programs that allow you to search a disk for defects. A ProDOS block is 512 bytes of data, and a standard Apple disk contains 280 such blocks. Remember that a byte is roughly equivalent to one character in a file. DOS 3.3 used 256-byte sectors, so a file in DOS 3.3 requires only half as many ProDOS blocks to hold it. The ProDOS Filer can also show how many blocks are available, how many are used, and how many are free. Another function of the Filer is the "Compare Volumes" function, which checks to see whether two different volumes are identical.

ProDOS has its dark side, though. Integer BASIC is not supported by this operating system. While most people won't miss Integer, its adherents are sure to be disappointed. For those who have been used to calling a slot and drive under DOS 3.3, be advised that your ability to do this is greatly limited under ProDOS. You must call for the name of the volume in order to address it.

Rule One in working with computers is to make second, or "backup", copies of the files on your disks. That's true of both program and data files, all of which are electronic versions of the paper files you would keep in a filing cabinet. If you lost all of the files in a filing cabinet, it would have a serious negative effect, which is why most people store valuable documents and records in safe deposit boxes and other places. That's particularly true in a business situation, of course, but it's no less valid for personal files in which you have many hours invested. Some computer sales people, trying to sell a computer that can't have more than one disk drive, have alleged that backing up disks wasn't important in the home situation. Tell that to the stamp or recipe collector whose data has just turned into hash.

In the ProDOS system supplied with your //c, the Filer program contains a program for copying one volume onto another, in addition to the program that lets you copy individual files. Use them and take the time to make your backup disks and files. If anybody tells you that data or program backup disks aren't important, or aren't worth the bother, or are a nefarious plot to sell you more blank disks, just smile and walk away from that person. Walk quickly. The backup disk copies are your insurance against disaster.

ProDOS is only now becoming available to the individual user, but it has been in the hands of software developers since late 1983. You may never need (or want) to know just which operating system is controlling your Apple at the moment, except when you are formatting data disks or working directly with files on those disks. So, an exhaustive discussion of ProDOS will not be undertaken here.

The Sockets on the Back

There's a row of sockets (which the cognoscenti call "connectors," "interfaces," or "ports") on the back of the //c for plugging in the cords that connect the //c to the outside world. Let's briefly identify each one right now. The job is made easier by the graphic symbols that appear above the sockets.

We'll work from right to left (with the back of the machine toward you). We have already discussed the 7-pin DIN connector where 15-volt power enters the unit from the power supply. It's on the far right. Next over is a socket that is round like the power socket. It takes a plug with five pins, not seven. This socket is called Serial Port 1, and it is normally used for connecting a printer or plotter. Previous Apple models did not use this round, 5-pin style of plug and socket, so you and your dealer

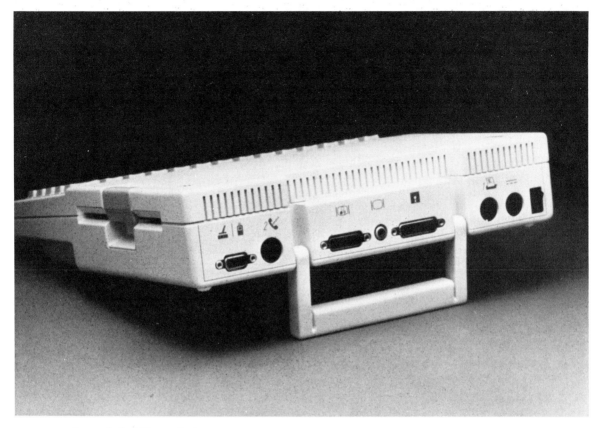

*Icons label the sockets
on the back.*

will have to make sure that you have the proper adapter
cords and fittings for the printer, plotters, and other
devices that you will be using. Apple is packaging interface kits for many popular peripherals.

Left of Serial Port 1 is a 19-pin D-type connector used
to attach your second disk drive. A "D-type" connector
is so named because if you look at it with its longer side
to your left, it looks like a narrow capital *D*. On the //c,
and on most peripherals used with it, the long side is on
top when the connector is plugged in.

Two sockets for connecting video displays are next.
The round, single-pin RCA-type socket is the one used

most often. As the video screen symbol or icon shows, a color or black-and-white video monitor will connect directly here. If you use a standard TV set, you'll need to use one other item, an RF modulator. This is a small box that converts your computer's output into a signal your TV can receive through its antenna terminals. Once the RF modulator is hooked up between the computer and the TV (a simple task), you can choose between TV and computer by flipping a small switch located on the modulator box. An RF modulator is packed with every //c (that's something new for Apple; previously, RF modulators were sold separately).

One note: in most hotels and motels, television sets are thoughtfully provided so that the maids can keep up with the soap operas while cleaning. It will not be uncommon for travelling businesspeople to hook up their //c's to these sets (using the RF modulators) for work and/or recreational color displays. If you want to hook up your //c, check with the hotel management first. Because theft is a problem, many hotel and motel TVs have electronic interlocks and signal devices that trigger alarms if the TV set is tampered with. What that means is that if you disconnect the TV antenna to hook up your RF modulator your room could very shortly look like a scene from Hill Street Blues.

Next to the RCA connector is a 15-pin D-type connector. That's a more complex audio and video connector, for advanced display devices. The most common device to be connected to this socket is likely to be the flat-panel LCD screen display, although sophisticated "RGB"-type color monitor adapters for the //c also plug in here. If you buy something that plugs into this socket, make sure the manual for that particular product explains how to make the connection. Also make sure that the peripheral is compatible with the //c. WARN-ING: this socket is not the same electrically as the 15-pin connectors used on other Apple models. Before hooking any device to this port, check with your dealer to avoid damage to your //c and/or the peripheral.

We now come to another 5-pin DIN connector, which looks just like Serial Port 1. In fact, it looks so much like Serial Port 1 that it's called Serial Port 2. It is marked by an icon or symbol showing a telephone handset. Serial Port 2 is normally used to connect your //c to a box-shaped device called a "modem" (MOdulator-DEModulator). Modems are used to connect computers to telephone lines; see Chapter Eight of this book for more information.

On the far left is the 9-pin D-type connector for hand controls. As the adjacent icons show, these controls can be paddles, a joystick, or even a mouse. The //c has built-in circuitry for the mouse. To use the mouse on other Apple // and /// models you'd need an extra aux-illiary circuit card plugged into one of the expansion slots. (Note again the beauty of the //c: if we were using an older model, we'd just about have all of the expansion slots filled by now.)

Now let's consider what's not there. Earlier Apple computers could accept a peripheral card that allowed you to connect a "parallel" mode communications device to the machine. The //c has no parallel output port, so only "serial" devices can be connected to it. Apple's current serial-only philosophy is also reflected in the Macintosh computer. Make sure that the external devices you use are configured for serial data transmission, not parallel. Chapter Eight covers this in more detail.

The //c is missing two sockets that were standard on other Apple models: the tape cassette input and output jacks. These jacks connected these older computers to the audio cassette recorders that were used for data storage in the early days before disk drives became available. Since the //c contains a built-in disk drive, the cassette port became expendable. Those of us who remember struggling with the problems of using tape cassettes, such as long and anxious waits to see if the program or data would actually load, won't miss them. If you are just now getting your first computer, you won't miss them either. The Apple world has long since outgrown tape cassettes, even though some manufacturers of low-end computer brands still use them.

The Handle

While you're using the //c the handle may be in the folded position so that the computer sits flat on the desk, table, or your lap. The handle may also be turned down 180 degrees and used as a brace to slant the keyboard up from your work surface. If you are far from home and forced to use a tabletop that is the usual 30 inches high, instead of the normal typing desk height of 27 inches, this additional feature will allow you a better typing angle. It will be especially appreciated if you're a touch typist. Even at the normal desk height, the use of the handle in its extended and lowered position will give a more normal slant to the keyboard. Movement of the handle is interfered with by whatever cords are plugged into the external disk drive or video sockets, and vice versa. Disconnect these cords before moving the handle, or move the handle before plugging in these items.

The Speaker

The built-in speaker will never win any high-fidelity prizes, but it sounds off well despite its 1 1/2-inch size. (It's about half the size of the speaker in the Apple //e.) The //c's speaker arrangement is a considerable improvement over the ones in earlier Apples. First, there is a volume control on the left side of the computer to adjust the sound level The //c also comes with earphones that can be used when you want to hear the computer's beeps but do not want to disturb other people nearby.

These earphones plug into the mini-jack adjacent to the volume control. An audio output line in the 15-pin socket on the back of the //e can be used to connect the audio signal to an external device.

And IBM's PCjr?
It's inevitable that the Apple //c is going to be compared with IBM's PCjr, although the //c is, in fact, even more powerful than some configurations of IBM's larger PC. The //c and PCjr are not compatible, and they use different microprocessor chips. The suggested list prices of the //c and IBM PCjr Extended Version are about the same ($1300), at least at this writing. It is not really fair to compare the //c and the $800 entry-level PCjr because the entry-level PCjr does not contain comparable features and is not likely to be taken seriously.

The //c represents a "compressed" version of the larger Apple //e. The PCjr is not a compressed version of IBM's popular PC, and the most popular PC disk operating systems (DOS 1.1 and DOS 2.0) will not work on the PCjr. The Apple //c uses the same operating systems as its larger cousins.

The PCjr is severely limited because only one disk drive can be used with the system. The PCjr's disk drive will store more than twice as much information as can be stored with the //c, but the lack of an optional second drive will lead to much disk-swapping by PCjr users.

The //c keyboard is the standard Apple //e design, and is built into the unit. The PCjr has a detached keyboard that uses an infra-red link (like many TV remote control devices) to send data to the computer. The PCjr keyboard, with its oddly shaped keys, has been a disappointment to many who have tried it. At least one company is planning to introduce a "better" keyboard for the PCjr, but to get it, you will pay extra. Other extra-cost items only on the PCjr are the batteries for the keyboard, cables, and the RF modulator. Both the PCjr and the //c use external power supplies.

Comparison of IBM PCjr and Apple //c

	PCjr (entry)	PCjr (extended)	//c (all)
Price	$800	$1300	$1300
Keys	62	62	63
Memory, standard	64K	128K	128K
Memory, limit	128K	128K	128K
Disk drives, standard	0	1	1
Disk drives, maximum	1	1	2
Disk capacity	--	360K	143K
Serial ports	1	1	2
Parallel port	1	1	0
Built-in speaker	No	No	Yes
Audio connection	Yes	Yes	Yes
Joystick connection	Yes	Yes	Yes
Mouse connection	No	No	Yes
Cassette tape interface	Yes	Yes	No
Hard disk capability	No	No	*
Monitors supported:			
Monochrome (80 col.)	No	No	Yes
Color (80 col.)	Yes	Yes	Yes
Color TV	Yes	Yes	Yes
Modem available	??	Yes	Yes
Compatible w/existing DOS of company's larger machine	No	No	Yes
Compatible with existing software	No	Some	Most
Approx. weight	12 lbs	16 lbs	7.5 lbs

TABLE 3-1

* - See your dealer

Table 3-1 gives some comparisons. What no table can show is that the //c as it comes can run more existing software "as is" than the PCjr. At bottom, it's quite literally an apples and oranges comparison. The PCjr, even as its limitations are becoming more widely known, could be preferred by some people whose computer environment is in the IBM PC, MS-DOS world. However, for use in the home, for education, or for travellers, the Apple //c will not be "outgrown" as quickly.

What the //c Can't Do

The //c cannot tell time. The Lisa, Macintosh, and the Apple /// Plus have built-in clock/calendar chips. The same capability can be had with an additional circuit board (e.g., the Thunderclock) in a II Plus or //e.

The //c cannot use programs with the CP/M operating system. Like the clock, that capability requires a separate board in an expansion slot similar to those found in the //e or Apple ///. (The Lisa and Macintosh are also incapable of using CP/M.)

The //c is limited to 128K of memory and no expansion is possible. Yes, there are rumors that when larger memory chips become available at reasonable prices, the whole thing will be upgradable, but that's (a) not con-firmed, and (b) in the future. How far in the future is anybody's guess. Note that we're not talking about technological advancement here, but, rather, about the uncertain forces of the marketplace.

As noted, there is no parallel port on the //c. This means that many models of printers will not be accom-modated. This is not likely to bother you unless you already have one of these parallel printers.

All of these things are more or less important, depend-ing on your needs. Many computer users will never use all of the available RAM memory, nor will they feel the effects of the //c's strict hardware limits. The Apple //e, however, will do the things that the //c will not, thanks to its expandability.

Now let's take a closer look at working with the //c, including its keyboard, the mouse, and much more.

4

Using the //c

The manuals and interactive disks that come with the Apple //c offer the best approach to learning about your new machine. Apple has put much time and effort into their preparation. The best advice that we can offer is to take the time to go through them step by step. This is important even if the //c isn't your first computer, or even if it isn't your first Apple. It's very tempting to turn the thing on and jump in. The people who do that are quite often the same people you hear three months later saying, "I didn't know it could do that, too!"

The Apple tutorials include screen displays that simulate the subject program's actual screen display in order to teach certain specific points. In most cases, the tutorial program will only accept one action or response from you — with an actual program, you'll have more choices available at any given time. For the tutorial, just follow the instructions exactly and don't experiment.

Rather than merely duplicating the tutorial material, this chapter will highlight the new or different features of the //c, beginning with a quick look at its keyboard.

Keyboards   Your Apple //c has a standard, full-size, 63-key keyboard. Despite the small overall size of the //c, there is no compromise here. The keyboard dimensions and layout are identical to those on all Apple models now being manufactured. For the Apple ///, //e, Lisa, Macintosh, and //c, the keyboards also follow the IBM Selectric standard.

The II Plus keyboard is similar to the Teletype keyboard, which was the keyboard most used by computer hobbyists in 1975. Placement of letters and numbers on this Apple keyboard is not different from a standard keyboard, but only capital letters, numbers and some punctuation marks could be typed from the Apple II keyboard. Since no lower-case letters could be used, the SHIFT key was not operable for case changes. Many II Pluses were modified by adding lower-case character generators and shift-key modification wires. With the current Apple computer line, these improvements are built-in.

The //e and //c have the following characters not found on the Apple II Plus keyboard:

OPEN APPLE, SOLID APPLE, UP and DOWN ARROWS, CAPS LOCK, TAB, and DELETE.

The OPEN APPLE and SOLID APPLE keys are also wired to operate like the pushbuttons on the game paddles, so you can play games without having to connect paddles to your computer. The UP ARROW, TAB and DELETE keys will operate properly only if the software you're running was programmed to "know" that they are there. CAPS LOCK, as the name implies, locks out lower-case letters, so that only capital letters are sent to the screen. If CAPS LOCK is in its *down* position, only CAPITALS can be typed. If CAPS LOCK is in its *up* position the SHIFT key operates normally, and either upper- or lower-case letters can be typed. You still must depress the SHIFT key to attain the upper symbol on a

The QWERTY Keyboard

non-letter key.

The Apple II Plus's REPEAT Key has been replaced by an automatic repeat feature on the //c. Any key function will begin to repeat if you hold a key down for about a second.

If you're a touch typist used to the old II Plus keyboard, you will have to learn the new positions of the following characters on the //c keyboard:

The //c's keyboard will also let you type all of the 128 characters in the American Standard Code for Information Interchange (ASCII) character set. The ASCII code was devised to be a uniform standard code; it's described in Chapter 7. The complete list of ASCII characters appears at the back of this book.

RESET   The RESET key on the //c is the parallelogram-shaped key located in the upper left corner of the keyboard. Because pressing RESET will have catastrophic effects on a running program, the //c requires you to simultaneously press the CONTROL key and the RESET key in order for a RESET command to be obeyed. The //c wants to be sure that you really wanted to press RESET.

Simultaneously pressing the trio of CONTROL, OPEN APPLE, and RESET will restart the system at any time — just as if you had turned off the power and then turned it back on. But, make sure you first push down the CONTROL and OPEN APPLE keys; then, while holding those two keys down, push the RESET button. Let go of all three keys when the computer disk drive begins to operate. The //c has this restart procedure because it doesn't produce the harmful (to the machine) electrical surges that occur when the computer is reset by actually turning the power supply off and on.

Sholes or Dvorak?

The //c's sold in the United States have a switch to change from the standard Sholes or "QWERTY" keyboard arrangement to the Dvorak keyboard. It's the rightmost one of the two, narrow switches located above and to the left of the keyboard, next to the RESET key. The narrow switches are best operated with a pointed instrument. (Don't use a pencil; graphite chunks can be hazardous to the //c's health.) If the switch is up, it's set for Sholes; if the switch is down, it's set for Dvorak. What, you may ask, is a Dvorak keyboard? Or, for that matter, what the heck is a QWERTY? Well, listen, my children, and you shall hear the story of uppity women learning to do things better than they were supposed to!

When typewriters were first built, they had individual keys with letter images formed on the ends of long pieces of steel. A fan-shaped arrangement would allow each key to strike the ribbon and the paper in the center of the machine. In those days all of the typewriter parts were mechanically operated and moved slowly when pressed. The original design specified that the most frequently used letter keys had to be operated with the left hand, and that keys for letters that usually fell adjacent in common English words would not be placed near each other on the keyboard. This arrangement was an intentional effort to slow down the speed of the typists and prevent them from jamming two or more keys into the center of the platen. The name "QWERTY" comes from the letter names of the six keys at the left end of the top row of letter keys. Many women (particluarly left-handed women) overcame the slowness and continued to jam the typewriters by being too efficient. It took better designs to eliminate the sticking problem.

The Dvorak keyboard is arranged differently. As the drawing in Figure 4-1 shows, the most frequently used keys are placed in the center row. Because the keys are more conveniently placed, the Dvorak layout is more efficient and faster than the QWERTY. The Dvorak keyboard was largely ignored until recently, when it was revealed that the U.S. Speed Typing Champion was using one.

On the Apple //c, this arrangement is available by pressing the second switch to the indented position. If you do so, the keyboard layout will be as shown in Figure 4-1. You will have to pry up the keycaps gently and install them in their correct positions.

The International //c

On Apple //c models sold internationally (outside of the United States), pressing the keyboard selector switch down doesn't configure the keyboard in a Dvorak layout, but rather in one of several international keyboard layouts appropriate for the country in which the //c is sold. These keyboard layouts are complete with accents and special letter keys for the language of that country. With the switch up, the standard US Sholes keyboard is available.

The //c, like the //e, was designed to be an international machine rather than an adapted US model. In fact, international models of the //e computer have the keyboard selector switch built in (US models do not). Apple computer has developed a truly global and multicultural approach to its operations, as evidenced by the fact that most of the people in charge of the company's

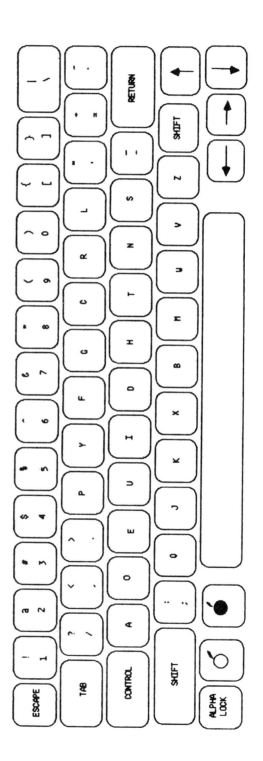

Figure 4-1

The Dvorak Keyboard

international program are not natives of the United States. Apple now offers Canadian, English, French, German, Italian, Spanish, and Western Spanish international keyboards.

Programming for the keyboard is stored in ROM. The configuration of each machine's keyboard ROM chip determines which keyboard the //c "thinks" it's addressing. If you're in the US, but believe that one of the bilingual keyboards would suit you better than a Sholes/Dvorak keyboard, ask your dealer to install the proper keyboard and chip. This will not be a free exchange, but it will be fairly simple to do. Apple has placed first priority on shipping the international keyboards to their "native" countries, but they do expect to have the conversion materials available for U. S. users.

Paddles and Joysticks

The keyboard is the primary mechanism for getting data into the computer. But for some applications, particularly games, other devices are much more desirable for sending control signals to the computer. (After all, everybody knows that spaceships are not flown with keyboards.) A variety of hand-held controllers has been devised to allow you to easily enter simple data, usually by turning a knob, pushing a button, or tilting a lever.

In their most primitive form, these game-type controllers take the form of twin "paddles," each with an adjustable control knob and a pushbutton. An image on the video screen can be moved up and down or back and forth with the knob controls, and the pushbuttons can fire a simulated space blaster or missile.

Some users prefer game-playing with "joysticks" instead of paddles. In the joystick the paddle knobs are replaced with a lever that can be moved back and forth and from side to side. Electronically, they perform the same function. The difference is that a simple joystick

The German Keyboard
Layout

replaces two paddles because the joystick's action in its vertical axis replaces one paddle control, and its action in the horizontal axis replaces the other paddle. Paddles and joysticks both have pushbuttons.

Paddles and joysticks plug into the //c at the 9-pin D-type connector, located at the left of the back panel. The paddles and joystick do not come with the computer. Caution: When you buy paddles or joysticks, make sure they have the 9-pin connector. Many older paddles and joysticks had a delicate 16-pin connector for the Apple II Plus. There is no place to plug in such a connector on the //c. Also, remember that the joysticks and paddles for your Apple are not likely to be compatible with those intended for another brand of computer, even if they look the same.

The Mouse

When Apple's Lisa was introduced, a primary feature of its architecture was the mouse. The mouse is a device that monitors the movement of someone's hand as they hold and move the mouse on a tabletop (excuse us, a desktop). This movement is directly translated into movement of the cursor on the screen. No up, down, or sideways arrow keys have to be pushed. A single button on the mouse is used to tell the computer that you want to change, select, or restore an entry.

The mouse, invented at Xerox PARC, was heralded as the best control device to come along since the on-off switch. The popularity of mice sold by Apple with the Lisa caused other manufacturers to come up with their own mouse devices. Some were so elaborate they had up to three pushbuttons on them. Apple was so over-whelmed by the response to the mouse that they decided to make mice available for every Apple model. To use a mouse with the II Plus, //e, or ///, a separate auxilliary board must be installed; but in the //c, the mouse "firmware" (ROM instruction set) is built in. The mouse

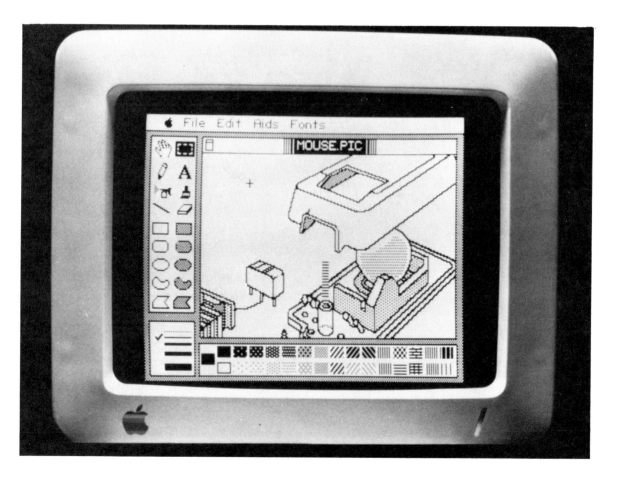

plugs into the paddle/joystick socket.

But, like all other peripheral devices attached to the computer, the mouse is no smarter than the software that controls it, so you must be using a software program that knows the mouse exists. Of the 20,000 programs that could now be used on the //c, comparatively few of them have instructions for controlling the mouse. Many programs are being updated, so this should be less of a problem in the future. To avoid being disappointed, you shouldn't invest in a mouse unless you also obtain mouse-related software, or you want to experiment and write your own programs. The MousePaint program comes with the mouse, and will get you started. In time, the mouse will be used for all types of data entry for business software as well as games.

At the risk of shattering some cherished illusions, we'll reveal that the mouse is functionally identical to a joystick or paddle. Movement of the mouse's internal ball as it rolls on the tabletop is measured along horizontal and vertical axes, and the mousebutton performs the same function as a paddle pushbutton. That does not mean that the mouse is interchangeable with the joystick. The two devices use different electrical connections.

For many people, the mouse has become addictive. It reflects the natural movements of your hand, and allows relaxed, positive control of the cursor. For those whose arms get tired from pointing at a screen (or brushing off the caterpillars), the mouse is preferred. Others, including many touch typists, think the mouse is an amusing toy but not essential to their work. Whether or not the mouse is the best form of data entry is purely a matter of taste. What's important is that the //c will accommodate your taste either way.

Video Displays   The keyboard is the //c's primary input device, and the video display is the primary output device. The video display doesn't provide a permanent record of the computer's output, but then, much (perhaps most!) of any computer's output isn't worth saving anyway.

To hook up a standard monochrome or color TV set to your //c, you'll need an RF modulator unit. But remember that you get only a 40-column display with a TV set. A black and white or NTSC color monitor can be hooked up directly to the RCA socket on the //c without the need for an RF modulator. You need a monochrome monitor for 80-column displays. The flat panel display, RGB color monitors, and other devices connect to the 15-pin video socket.

The //c allows you to tell it whether you have only 40-column, or 40- and 80-column, text-display capability on your video monitor. The switch you use to tell it is located between RESET and the Keyboard Selector (Sholes/Dvorak) switch. If the switch is up, the 40- /80-column display is selected; if the switch is down, the 40-column display mode is selected. Note that setting this switch does not automatically control the display. It merely sends a signal to those programs that check display status and tell the machine what kind of monitor is hooked up.

Four modes of display are available with the //c: *Text, Lo-Res graphics, Hi-Res graphics*, and *Double Hi-Res graphics*. In the text mode, you can produce a 24-line display of preset alphanumeric characters. Depending on the software you're using, you may have a display that has either 40 characters or 80 characters on a single line. In common with the //e, your Apple //c lets you choose from two character sets. Both character sets provide upper- and lower-case "normal" display, that is, white letters on a black or green screen. The standard character set also contains capital letters (no lower-case) when the computer is set in "inverse" mode (dark letters in a light block), or in "flashing" mode (alternating between normal and inverse display about four times a second). This character set is compatible with software written for the Apple II and Apple II Plus.

The second or alternate character set does not use the flashing upper-case letter set, but it does contain a lower-case inverse character set as well as the inverse capital letters. There is a disconcerting difference here between the //c and the //e. The //e has two sets of upper-case letters in its memory, and in the 80-column mode, either set consists of letters. Not so on the //c. As part of the mouse programming in the //c, one of the two sets of inverse capital letters has been replaced by a group of 32 graphics characters collectively known as Mousetext™. This difference can cause problems if you use a piece of software written for the //e but not updated for the //c. Some inverse text on the screen in 80-column mode may have funny squiggles instead of the capital letters. Do not adjust your computer; the problem is in the program, and it's not fatal to your software.

While we're on character sets, we would like to point out a significant advance involving lower-case letters that's new to the //c. You can program in BASIC (see Chapter 6) using lower-case as well as upper-case let-ters. On the Apple //e if you type a programming com-mand (such as RUN) in lower-case letters, the computer will not recognize it. Instead, it will return the dreaded SYNTAX ERROR ("you goofed") message. On the //c you may type BASIC commands in upper- or lower-case, or any combination of the two. The computer's Applesoft BASIC language interpreter program will recognize the command (so long as it is spelled correctly!). If you LIST (do a line-by-line display of) the program after you do this, you'll find that the commands have all been trans-lated into upper-case for display. DOS commands must still be entered as upper-case letters. For example, lower-case "pr#6" or "catalog" will cause an error message to be displayed.

Lo·Res Graphics   The first of the //c's three graphics modes is Woz's original color block matrix. The matrix, an imaginary grid displayed on the screen, is divided into 40 columns and 40 rows. Apple calls it a "Lo-Resolution" or "Lo-Res" graphics matrix. In *Lo-Res* mode, each color block in it can be any one of 16 colors, including white and black. On a black-and-white monitor, the blocks appear as shades of gray. Each color block is as wide as a single text character, and half as high. Two or more adjacent blocks of the same color appear as a larger shape, and there is no boundary line between blocks. Lo-Res graphics cannot generally be intermixed with text on the screen. The exception to this occurs when text appears on the 4 lines below the 20-line Lo-Res graphics page. These four lines are left for text display (such as titles) while the //c is in graphics mode.

Hi·Res Graphics   "Hi-Res" stands for "High Resolution" graphics. For *Hi-Res* mode, the matrix grid is not 40 rows by 40 columns as in color-block Lo-Res, but 192 rows by 280 columns. Each "block" is in fact one of the dots of light on the screen. The computer folks call this a "bit-mapped" screen because each dot of light has a corresponding bit somewhere in the computer's memory. Think of a bit as an electronic switch that can be either on or off. If that bit is "clear," or off, the dot is unlit (off). If the bit is "set," or on, the dot is lighted (on). With colors, it's a bit more complicated than that, but you get the idea. To take care of all of the dots and colors, a Hi-Res "page" of material requires 8K of memory just to control the image on the screen.

Hi-Res graphics allow six colors: black, white, purple, green, orange, and blue. Much software has been written for Hi-Res, and some of that software allows you to blend dots in order to have more than six colors. Hi-Res graphics have sold many people on Apple II computers.

Double Hi-Res Graphics

The *Double Hi-Res* graphics mode is similar to the standard Hi-Res mode, but provides a 192-row by 560-column display. The greater number of dots allows greater detail in images created by using this graphics mode. Double Hi-Res is available on Apple's //c, //e, and /// Plus computers, and requires software that has been designed to take advantage of it.

In the next chapter, we'll explore the four, most-often-cited answers to the question, "What do you use your Apple for?" (Or, in the educational field, "For what do you use your Apple?")

5

The Four Most-Used Functions

If you bought your new //c at the behest, nay, nagging of your children or because someone made you feel guilty that your kids were being left behind in the great technological world, you probably already have some idea of the most-used functions of a personal computer: playing games. After all, isn't that what the kids have been doing with it ever since you brought it in the door? Actually, that's probably your just desserts for all the years you gave the kids Christmas toys (like model trains), and they never got a chance to play with them!!

You don't have to be a kid to enjoy playing games, but would you want to admit to all your friends that that's what you're doing with this machine that is supposed to be able to do everything but the dishes and the windows? Let's find out about three of the "adult" things that you can do with it, and then you can dazzle your friends with the speed of your machine. We'll get back to games, too.

The three (remaining) most often cited functions of computers are: (1) word processing, (2) data base management, and (3) spreadsheet analysis. Well, are those just fancy words that the computer types invented to keep the discussion "in the family?" Not really, although their jargon can get a bit confusing. Let's look at these functions one at a time, first generally, and then more specifically. Because there are so many different software products on the market for these functions, we'll zero in on one recently introduced product that integrates or combines all three.

Word Processing

Word processing is really moving words around. In the old days, it was called typewriting, or in even older days, just plain "writing." But remember what you had to do in your school days (or still have to do, if you're in school)? To write a paper, you first wrote a rough draft, scribbled lots of notes in the margin, marked it up for your footnotes, did a second draft, checked for spelling errors, did a third draft, etc., etc., etc. Always lurking just over your shoulder was the dreaded typographical error. The worst "typos" were those that occurred in corrected copies. You would fix one error, but another would pop up. Result: Type it all again, Sam.

Enter the //c and a word processor program that will let you type the letter, paper, or other document on the screen. Correct your mistakes by deleting and retyping only the offending characters. Move words, sentences, even paragraphs around until you get the document right. All of this is done electronically, without eraser, scissors, and pastepot. Once you're finished (and even at strategic points during the process) you can store the document on a disk. If you have a printer, you can generate a "hard copy" on paper.

The main advantage of the word processor is that you don't have to retype all the material from the beginning each time you make corrections. You can insert material that started out as notes in the margins. You can delete errors and bad writing, and the remaining text closes up to hide the deletion. You can also insert superscripted numbers for your footnotes.

Depending upon the abilities of the particular word-processing program that you use, you may also be able to change type faces for your printer, automatically format the pages complete with footnotes, and browse through the material on the screen to verify the format before you print your document out on paper. Do you want another copy? Just send it to your printer again.

Is it hard to learn to "word-process?" Not really, especially if you think about the time you spent learning to write and/or type before you became competent with those skills. Give yourself some time to become familiar with the commands and techniques of your word processor and you will soon find that it seems old-fashioned to insert a page or an envelope into your typewriter!

Data Base Management

Data base management is the computer equivalent of taking all those bits and pieces of paper off your desk, filing them neatly away in properly labeled folders, and then placing the folders in a file drawer. On the computer, however, you can search your files for a number of different records ("pieces of paper") that have something in common. Once the correct files are located, the data base program will display them on the screen for you, or if you prefer, print a list of the selected records on the printer. You don't have to remember in which drawer the records were filed; the computer will do the looking for you with the speed of light, and it won't leave the folders all over the place afterwards!

Funny thing about the speed of light and computer searches. The computer will search and find records in a few seconds, a process that would take much longer to find by hand if they were on papers. After you get used to the computer, you will begin to suffer from impatience. You will begin to say that a computer search taking more than twenty seconds is "slower than molasses." Never mind that it used to take three hours by hand. Once we have something, we want more of it.

Spreadsheets

How many times have you had to work with a page of columns and rows of numbers that needed to be added, subtracted, or multiplied? You're probably familiar with an out-of-balance checkbook, a budget (by month and by category) that's almost in balance, or a list of bills that needs to be added to see if enough money is in the checkbook. You have also probably accumulated many pounds of eraser shavings getting things to add up across as well as down. With an "electronic spreadsheet" your Apple //c can automatically do a lot of this number work.

The electronic spreadsheet is a program that creates and displays on the screen a matrix or grid of boxes. In each of these boxes you can put a label (e.g., "Sales"), or a numeric value (e.g., "100"), or a formula (e.g., "Sales - Cost"). You design the "worksheet" (the displayed page you're working on) for the job you want done. With proper planning, you can use the program to design a worksheet that will let you change your number entries and see what will happen to your budget! You can play "What if. . . ." For example, suppose your formulas assume a 6 per cent annual growth rate. What if it were seven per cent? Change just the percentage entry. The spreadsheet program will recalculate the worksheet and display the new values on the screen. It's always good to see that you don't have enough money to buy that Rolls Royce before you get into the showroom.

Integrated Software

During the past year, there has been a new development in software. Previously, you had to have separate software programs on separate disks for different functions. So you had a separate word processor, a data base, and a spreadsheet. Data generated by one program was not readily available to another. Further, to go from one program to another, you had to reboot the system, which meant you did a lot of disk swapping. Also, you could not easily take a pertinent segment of a spreadsheet worksheet or data base printout and enter them into a report being written on the word processor.

Apple's Lisa was one of the first computers to offer an integrated "desktop" software approach, that allows information interchange between data bases, spreadsheets, and the word processor. The Lisa is an integrated operating system. Lotus Development took another tack with its "1-2-3," a single program that contains a text processor function and a simple data base management ability — all within an overall spreadsheet program. The 1-2-3 program is not available for the Apple //c.

With integrated software packages you can switch from one application to another without having to reboot your whole system, and you can simultaneously work with several data files. Sometimes you must record or save a file to disk in an ASCII file format instead of the program's own format in order to make it compatible with the program, but this is a small price to pay for the great conveniences these integrated programs offer. Now there are several integrated software packages available for the Apple 6502 family computers, including Apple's own AppleWorks for the //e and //c, and "3 EZ Pieces" (identical to AppleWorks) for the Apple ///.

We will use Apple's Appleworks integrated software to give you some introductory examples. If your programs are different ones, the examples will still work, but some of the keyboard or mouse commands may be different.

Using the Software

The first thing you should do, if your program(s) will allow it, is to make copies of your original program disks. Once this is done, store the original disks in a safe place and use the copies. That way, you will always be able to make a new daily-use copy from the original if, perish the thought, something happens to a disk with which you work every day.

Some program disks have been altered by their manufacturers so that you cannot easily make a copy. The reason that manufacturers "copy-protect" their products is simple. They don't want them stolen. And it *is* stealing to pass along unauthorized copies of software to others. It's also stealing for a company to buy one copy of a program and then make copies for its 37 branches in four states.

But it is not improper or illegal for you to retain copies of software that you legitimately purchased, for your own use or for your archives. If you can get backup program disks at a reasonable cost from the software manufacturer or your dealer, fine. If not, buy software from a more reasonable manufacturer. Also, other manufacturers make programs that copy the "uncopyable" altered disks. You can legally develop the capability to make your own backup copies of the programs you use.

AppleWorks comes with five disks; the start-up or boot disk, the program disk, two introductory disks, and a sample file disk. Take the time to go through the tutorial disks and get to know the program. Boot the start-up disk and wait for the displayed instruction telling you to insert the program disk. Once this happens, insert the program disk and press «RETURN». Then enter the date, press «RETURN» again, and you're off. You will see the "main menu", appearing on the face of what looks like a file folder; as you work through to other functions, each will be identified by its own file folder picture.

It might be more convenient for you to copy the program to one side of a blank disk for daily use, and copy the boot ("system start-up") to the other side of the same disk. Most 5-1/4-inch disks have a notch cut in the jackets. If that notch is unobstructed, you can record on that disk. If the write-enable notch is covered, you can only read from that disk. By carefully cutting a second write-enable notch in the opposite side of the one already cut in the disk jacket, you can copy to the back side of a floppy disk. Caution: Do not attempt to cut this second write-enable notch unless you're sure of what you are doing. Try it with a blank disk and expendable data file copies first. Then, when the disk is inserted upside down, the Apple disk drive will write (record) on the back side of the disk. To start Appleworks, boot from the back side, and flip the disk to the program side when you are instructed to do so.

Some folks will give you thirteen reasons for not using the back of a disk. There is the possibility that the back side may be flawed. Well, if the back is flawed, it'll become apparent when you boot the system. If it is flawed, use another disk. We recommend that the program disk side be the front, because it is used much more than the boot section. There is also the certainty that cutting that second notch will void the warranty on the disk. Since disks cost less than $5 each, that's not likely to worry many people.

The first thing to do is to get the file or files you want from a disk, or to start new files. If this is your first entry into the program, choose the "Add files to the Desktop function", which should be highlighted. All you need to do is press «RETURN». You will then be presented with a second menu, in a second file folder graphic, called "Add Files". Note that Appleworks allows you to work on more than one file at a time on your "electronic desktop".

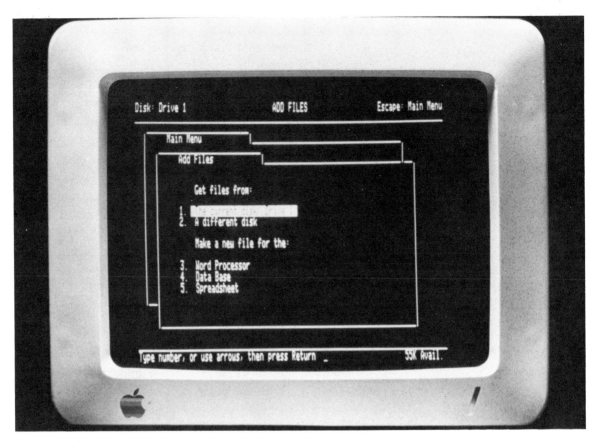

The "ADD FILES" Display

For this first go, we'll start a new file. Move the screen highlight with the down arrow key to "Word Processor" (or type in the number 3) to select the proper function. Then press «RETURN». You will be asked to give a name to the document (how about "Letter1"?); press «RETURN» after typing in the name and you will then be presented with an almost blank screen which is your "paper". Start typing. See? It really works!!

The Word Processor

Suppose that you want to type a letter. Follow the directions outlined above, or in your manual, for starting a new word processor file. You should have a blank (or almost blank) screen. As soon as you begin typing, you'll see the words appear on the screen, just as if it were a fresh sheet of paper. The information at the top (and sometimes at the bottom) of the screen tells you things such as the name of the file you are working with, the location of the cursor (how far across the line or how far into the current paragraph you are), and possibly the current length of the file and/or the space remaining in memory.

The AppleWorks program is set up to allow you 79 characters (letters, spaces, numbers, whatever) across the screen. As you type, notice that the program will keep a word that would go beyond the right margin "all in one piece" by moving it down to the next line. You don't have to worry about a bell ringing, and you don't have to press the carriage return lever to advance the paper. Keep typing until you want to start a new paragraph. Then press «RETURN» to move the cursor down one line -- press it twice if you want to double-space between paragraphs. You will notice at the bottom of the screen that the program is keeping track of how many lines you have typed and the position of the cursor on the page.

If you have been typing in the sample letter (Letter1), you have noticed that each new line starts at the far left of the page. Don't worry about margins yet; we'll take care of them when we print the letter. You can type your letter with every line starting flush with the left margin, which may be the easiest way to start until you are familiar with the operation of your word processing pro-gram. This format is called "full block", but is not the one we generally use in writing letters. You can make it look more like a regular letter by using the TAB key to move the cursor a pre-defined number of spaces across the screen. Check your manual to find out what value has been set for the TAB spacing. For example, using AppleWorks, the default (preset) value is every five

24 April 1984

Dear Aunt Minnie,

I know you will want to share my excitement about my new "toy"
which I have just purchased. Actually, the Apple //c computer is
not a toy, but a wonderful machine which will allow my to do many
things that have fascinated my for a long time.

It is a nice, light-weight, portable computer which has many
wonderful features built-in. Some people think that I say so much
that is nice about the //c that I must work for Apple Computer
Inc. but it's really just because I find it so much fun to work
with.

I want to thank you for the generous birthday gift which made all
this possible, and I couldn't think of a better way to write to
you than to use the Apple //c and the Appleworks software
package.

Thanks again for your generosity.

Love,

Julie

Letter 1

spaces. Using AppleWriter //, the default value is every eight spaces.

If you write a reasonably short letter, you can probably wait and save it to your data disk when you have finished typing. If you write an annual treatise, you should make it a habit to save the document periodically while writing it. Saving long documents to a disk every fifteen minutes or so is just insurance, in case the unthinkable happens, such as a monster thunderstorm that cuts off the power to your computer! To save your in-process AppleWorks document, press «OPEN-APPLE» and S simultaneously; the program will save the document to your data disk and return the screen to you. The cursor will be just where it was when you left off, so that you can continue typing without having to find your place. Note that with only one disk drive, you'll be asked to insert the data disk in the drive for this. Then, you'll swap disks again to replace the program disk.

Ooops! You say you don't have a data disk handy? Fortunately, the folks who designed this program (and any other well-designed program, regardless of the application) remembered that just this might happen and have given you a lifeline. When the screen says "Insert Data Disk" and you don't have one, press the ESCape key to get back to the main menu. Select choice 5 (Other Activities) from the main menu. A new second menu will appear. Select number 5 (Format a blank disk) from this second menu. A new set of directions will appear. Follow the directions to create a disk that will accept your letter. Remember this process, because there'll come a time when the text you are working on will not be saved because your data disk is full. AppleWorks is designed so that the formatting process will not cause the computer to forget what was in your letter; it will still be there on the desktop — even though it may not be immediately visible on the screen. You can

24 April 1984

Dear Aunt Minnie,

I know you will want to share my excitement about my new
"toy" which I have just purchased. Actually, the Apple //c
computer is not a toy, but a wonderful machine which will allow
my to do many things that have fascinated my for a long time.

It is a nice, light-weight, portable computer which has many
wonderful features built-in. Some people think that I say so much
that is nice about the //c that I must work for Apple Computer
Inc. but it's really just because I find it so much fun to work
with.

I want to thank you for the generous birthday gift which
made all this possible, and I couldn't think of a better way to
write to you than to use the Apple //c and the Appleworks
software package.

Thanks again for your generosity.

Love,

Julie

Letter 2

recall it when you're through with the formatting process.

You have now learned to type text, reposition it using the TAB key, and then to save it. But what if you wanted a second letter (see Letter2) similar to the first but with different margins? To do this, all you need do is call up Letter1 on the screen. Once it is visible, you can use the TAB key to rearrange the margins. Here's how:

Press Open-Apple and T (for TAB) to get the options for TABs at the bottom of the screen; move the cursor using the left and right arrows to the location where you want your TAB stop, and press S for set. You may set as many tab stops as you wish before pressing the ESC key to return to the typing screen. You could even set a tab stop at every column position if you wanted! (But I don't think you'd want to, do you??)

Using the TAB key, you can move the cursor so that you are positioned to type the date and return address to the right of center of the screen. When you press the RETURN key to move to the next line, you will be at the left again so you can decide if you want to start typing there or use the TAB to move across the screen again. After you have typed the body of the letter, you can use the TAB key to place the closing under the return address.

Later, when you are more comfortable with the commands of your word processor, you can set printing formats from within the program, using the Options menu. It will pay you to spend some time learning about the way to include printer commands for margins, bold face, italics, and underlining. Some word processors (e.g., AppleWriter //) will also let you position footnotes at the bottom of the page on which the reference occurs. Others (including AppleWorks) will allow you to make footnote references, even using superscripted numbers, but will require that you have the actual footnotes at the end of the document.

A word processor is best used in creating documents that are formatted in paragraphs. You can type tables of figures but it will probably be easier to create your tables with either the data base or spreadsheet program. If you are using an integrated program like AppleWorks, you can cut the table from the database and insert (or "paste") this table into your word processing document — all without having to start up an entirely new program.

The Data Base Program

A data base program is an electronic filing system, used for organizing, storing, and locating information. Data base management programs work with the kind of information found on cards in file drawers, but the computer's way is much faster and more convenient.

You must think a little bit before you start designing your computerized file cabinet, just as you would to set up a filing system with folders and pieces of paper. What categories do you want to have? Which method will you want to use for organizing your files, alphabetical or numerical? The real advantage to a computerized data base is that you can quickly locate sub-categories of information, based on selected criteria, e.g., current customers in Oregon with last names beginning with J.

Data base programs use two kinds of methods for handling files: memory-based and disk-based. A memory-based program loads an entire file into your //c's memory, where it works on the whole thing. A disk-based program holds "key" or "pointer" files in memory, but not all of the data. Disk-based programs can store information about more items because they're not limited by the computer's memory. But memory-based programs can find and sort the data in far less time because everything is in one place. Memory-based programs (of which AppleWorks is one) are generally easier to use.

With the //c, AppleWorks leaves more than 50K bytes of memory available for one or more data files on your desktop. This translates into roughly a thousand or more record entries, depending on the size of each record.

As an example of how a data base-management program works, let's build a file catalog of your (hypothetical) music collection. You may have both phonograph records and tapes, some with many titles and some with only a single title. You may want to have categories such as composer, title, and an index number for each record or tape. The number would correspond with a label you place on the record or tape. Numbering your records might make them easier to locate when you want to play your favorite record for a friend. Numbering is not a new idea — we have been using it for library books since Melvil Dewey invented his Decimal System.

The word "category" in AppleWorks, by the way, corresponds to what old hands with data base-management programs know as "fields". It works this way: A file of your customers contains a record for each customer. Each customer record contains fields or categories with items of information about that customer. For example, Telephone Number would be a *field* or category in the Jones *record*.

Back to phonograph records, each of which would have a corresponding computer record. What else do we want to know? How about a category or field for the performer's name, and another for the type of music? Maybe one for the date you purchased a particular piece. You could include your own "ratings" or a personal category relating to moods. In addition, you may wish to indicate the length of the piece (if you are planning to use the music for background in making your own videotape program, for example), a Kirschel listing number if you are a Mozart fan, or any other miscellaneous information.

An alternative filing system for your albums is to file them alphabetically by artist. You may want categories for size/type; e.g., 12-inch, cassette, 7-inch, etc. The point is that data base "managers" like the one in AppleWorks let you make the system the way you want it, and even change it if you're not satisfied with the first try. Some earlier data base programs can't be modified after you have entered data, but AppleWorks can.

Once you have decided upon the categories you want, type in the category names (up to 30 of them) and then get down to the work of filling in the information for each category in each record. AppleWorks uses two screen display formats, one for an individual record and another for multiple records. You can enter data in either display format. You can also partially fill a record with common information, make copies of the record, and fill in the different information in each copy. If you have a very large collection of music, the time required to enter all this data may seem to be almost more than you want to spend. But just as you can develop a traditional paper-and-folder system a bit at a time, you can enter your information into the computer a little bit at a time. You save the file as it exists after each session, and later add items to the file at the point where you left off.

The benefit of using a data base-management program such as the one in AppleWorks is that the speed of finding and arranging your information offsets the work of data entry. In fact, the larger the mass of data, the more you will appreciate the electronic searching that your //c can do for you.

With the AppleWorks data base for example, you can search for those records in which any category equals, is less than, is greater than, contains, does not contain, begins with, or ends with, some stated value you enter. For example, "Find all records where 'Composer' contains 'Mozart', or "Find all records where 'Composer' contains 'Beethoven' and 'Artist' contains 'Phila.' Dates

```
File: music                    REVIEW/ADD/CHANGE            Escape: Main Menu

Selection: All records


Indx  Composer   Title             Label  No.      Performer       Type
====================================================================================
1     Mozart     Eine Kleine Nachtm Col    ML1329   Phila.          classic
6     —          YMCA              Verve  4572     Village People  rock
9     Kern       Show Boat         Col    ML840    Kostalenetz     Show inst
12    Anderson   Belle of the Ball RCA    LPS1859  Fiedler         Lt. Class
22    Joplin     Maple Leaf Rag    Epic   ES3382   Morath          ragtime
```

are handled specially by AppleWorks. For example, you can find all records where "Purchase Date" is after "May 2, 1981," and before "May 2, 1983". The //c will find the records meeting your specifications in seconds, or tell you if no records matching your specifications exist. You can also arrange your records with any of the categories listed in alphabetical or numerical order. If the category is a date, it can be arranged in chronological or reverse chronological order. You can then print out the rearranged list. You can even print a list of selected items using criteria such as those described above.

Once you have a list of your music collection stored on two disks (remember the backup disk) and find out how easy it is to search by composer, title, or some other criterion, you will begin to find other lists and collections that need to be organized. Also, you'll never again purchase a wonderful sounding item from your record club, only to find that you already had two or three copies of the same piece!

Your data base-management system will make it easy for you to organize your books, clippings, videotapes, Christmas-card and other mailing lists, or notes for speeches, or anything else that you want to organize. If you are a hobbyist, you might wish to have your Storybook Dolls, or stamps, or model railroad locomotives filed away in such a computerized data base. And the beauty of the data base is that it is so flexible. You can experiment, shift, add, delete, refine, and review your information framework.

The Spreadsheet

The electronic spreadsheet is probably the least familiar function of these three applications programs. A spreadsheet is typically a tool used in accounting, and not everyone is an accountant who works regularly on columnar pads with lots of little squares filled with numbers. Number manipulation, or "number crunching," in computerese, is what the spreadsheet (and the computer) does best. In fact, it was VisiCalc, the first electronic spreadsheet (primitive by today's standards), that helped fuel the microcomputer revolution. Let's take a look at what a spreadsheet is and see how it works. Later we can work with a sample.

Think of the spreadsheet as a large "sheet" of rows and columns. You can only see a part of the entire sheet on the screen at any one time. Imagine rows that extend across the screen from side to side. The rows are numbered down the left side of the screen, from 1 at the top to 254 or more at the bottom. The columns run from top to bottom of the sheet, and are lettered from Column A at the far left to 65 columns or more on the right. At each row-and-column intersection, there is a "cell" into which information may be entered. Each cell is known by its row-and-column coordinates. Cell A1 is at the upper-left corner of the sheet. Cell C5 is four rows below Cell A1 and two columns to the right.

Into any cell, you can enter either labels (words and/or symbols, with or without numbers) or values (numbers or formulas that result in numbers). Labels and numbers are straightforward data entries, such as "Sales," "Total," "Net Loss," "256," or "5.77." The formulas cause mathematical operations to be performed on the contents of other cells, with other values. For example, "A5 * 2" means that the contents of Cell A5 will be multiplied by 2. The asterisk is used to signify multiplication. And the formula "@SUM(F4 . . . F15)" for a cell means that it will contain the sum of all the values in those cells in Column F from Row 4 through Row 15. The formulas allow you to create a spreadsheet that can change totals and other values automatically when data is changed.

Column width is user-defined, which means that you may choose to have each column be from one to seventy or eighty characters wide. An extremely narrow column is probably useful only as a divider (a column of vertical lines, perhaps), while the extremely wide columns limit the view you have on the screen to few columns or a single column at once. For most applications, columns are usually nine or ten characters wide.

As we said, if you create a spreadsheet larger that your screen display, you can only see part of your work on the screen at any one time. The arrow keys let you move in any direction, and you can even split the screen to see two parts of your sheet at once.

If your spreadsheet program is like AppleWorks and allows variable width columns, you may wish to make the columns that will contain labels wider than those that will contain numbers, because most labels will be wider than the number entries. If you have an older spreadsheet program that does not allow variable widths, you will have to complete your desired labels in the adjacent column(s). If you need to have some type-written information in columnar form, you can even use the spreadsheet to list the data as labels in columns without any mathematical calculations.

```
File: cash record              REVIEW/ADD/CHANGE                 Escape: Main Menu
========A==========B===========C=============D============E=======
  1|
  2|
  3|      Expenses            Budget        Actual          Diff.
  4|
  5|      Housing              450           425             25
  6|      Utilities            100            90             10
  7|      Food                 100            95              5
  8|      Clothing              35            55            -20
  9|      Recreation            10             5              5
 10|      Savings               97            85             12
 11|      Taxes                 58            58              0
 12|                    ----------------------------------------------
 13|      Tl. Expenses         850           813             37
 14|                    ==============================================
 15|      Income              850           840            -10
 16|                    ----------------------------------------------
 17|      Net Variance                                       27
 18|
     ----------------------------------------------------------------
A1
```

```
File: cash record              REVIEW/ADD/CHANGE                 Escape: Main Menu
========A==========B===========C=============D============E=======
  1|
  2|
  3|      Expenses            Budget        Actual          Diff.
  4|
  5|      Housing      450     425           +C5-D5
  6|      Utilities    100      90           +C6-D6
  7|      Food         100      95           +C7-D7
  8|      Clothing      35      55           +C8-D8
  9|      Recreation    10       5           +C9-D9
 10|      Savings       97      85           +C10-D10
 11|      Taxes         58      58           +C11-D11
 12|                ----------------------------------------------
 13|      Tl. Expenses  @SUM(C5...C11)  @SUM(D5...D11)  @SUM(E5...E11)
 14|                ==============================================
 15|      Income        850     840           +D15-C15
 16|                ----------------------------------------------
 17|      Net Variance                +E15+E13
 18|
     ----------------------------------------------------------------
A1
```

In a variable-column spreadsheet program you could reduce the width of the first column and leave it blank. This will let you print out the information and save the page in a three-ring binder without having the punched holes in the paper interfere with any of your information.

For an example, let's build a simple cash-record document. Select the AppleWorks option to create a new document for the spreadsheet. You should now have a blank sheet on the screen. Use Column B for titles, and type in row names such as Income, Housing, Food, Clothing, Recreation, Savings, and Taxes. In Column C, enter the budget amounts allocated to the various categories. Column D will be reserved for entering the actual amounts spent (or earned, in the case of income), and Column E will have formulas that will show you whether you have kept within your budget or not! (Are you sure you want to know that??) The formula for Cell E5 would be stated as "C5 − D5," meaning that the number displayed in Cell E5 will be the value in Column C minus the value in Column D. If the result is negative, you should reduce your spending!

One of the best aspects of spreadsheetery is this: A label, value, or formula entered in one box or cell can be quickly copied or "replicated" to another cell or group of cells. In our example, you would type in the formula in cell E5 (Rows 1 to 4 have been reserved for titles, and Column A for the holes you are going to punch in the paper). Then, copy the contents of cell E5 into the cells from from E6 through E11.

If the cell or cells being copied contain a formula, there is a question as to how the formula will be copied. For example, if the "C5 − D5" formula in Cell E5 were copied with no changes, you would have the values from Row 5 used on each of the rows below. That's not what we want, of course. We want Cell E7, for example, to contain "C7 − D7," Cell E8 to contain "C8 − D8," etc. So when you copy (replicate) a formula, you will be given a choice for each item in that formula: "relative" or "no change." If "relative" is selected, the formula in the new cell will contain cell coordinates corresponding to the relative change in location between the original or source cell and the cell containing the copy.

A most efficient technique for using spreadsheets is to construct a "template" of labels and formulas, but omit any number values. The template is like a blank form. It can be saved to a disk file, and then recalled over and over for use with different sets of numbers. In our example, we could use the labels and formulas we entrered as a template, which could be used later for different data — without having to start from scratch.

Backup Data Disks

Didn't we cover backup disks in a previous chapter? Yes, and it's too bad we can't mention them on every page. Data backup isn't important until you have to spend hours re-entering data lost because of a power failure, static electricity, or some inexplicable electronic burp. Here, we're going to describe the backup process in more detail.

To make backup copies of your data files, you can save each file to a second disk when storing them. If you are using ProDOS, you can also use the ProDOS Filer to copy selected files from one disk to another or to copy an entire disk. If you are using DOS 3.3, the FID program copies files and the COPYA program copies entire disks. You will need a blank disk for each disk you wish to copy. Load the copy program into the computer memory and follow the instructions that appear on the screen. If you are only using one disk drive, you will have to swap the original for the copy disk every so often, as directed, because the computer can only store a limited amount of information at one time. When you have the disk copied, be sure to label it so you remember what is on it. Those black vinyl disk covers all tend to look alike after a while!

The best backup system actually involves three disks, not two. (No, we're not shilling for the disk manufacturers; read on!) Call the disks A, B and C. Let's assume that the data files are modified each day. So, Monday we use disk A and copy the data to B for the next update. Tuesday we use disk B and copy the data to C for the next day. Wednesday we use disk C and copy the data to A for the next day. What happens is that on any given day, if a problem occurs, we lose no more than one day's updates. And, if we have somehow transmitted that glitch to the next-day disk, we still have the third disk and we're no more than two days behind. That's better than starting from scratch. Some businesses use five disks, one for each workday. The lengths to which you want to go are dictated by how much the data is worth to you, or more precisely, how much its loss would affect you.

Games and Simulations

Now that we have covered the most common "serious" uses of your Apple //c, we can return for a look at a phenomenon of the 1980s: computer games. At one level, these are the electronic versions of pinball or arcade games. You test your eye-hand coordination by fending off or eliminating "attackers" of one kind or another. This process is usually accompanied by the *son et lumiere* of global war that emanates from the speaker and screen.

A higher level of gaming is the group of fantasy simulations. In these games, you are a warrior or adventurer with a mission to complete. That mission may be rescue, treasure recovery, conquest, solving a mystery, or just saving the world from destruction. In any case, you proceed through the program and live or die by the decisions you make along the way. The most popular of these are variations of Dungeon-type games. You search through the magic castle, find the treasure, and rescue the princess from the evil IBaMorph, or something.

An immense variety of these games has been placed on the market, in what seems almost a parody of the popular music record industry. Games "hit the charts," "make the Top Ten," and then fade away to be replaced by others. Most of the game writers are in, or not too long removed from, their teens, and began as hobbyists/hackers. Some of these programmers are being accorded "star" status by those in the industry who believe that such a process will help sales, or egos, or both. At any rate, the game designers have certainly advanced the state of the art in the field of computer graphics.

There is a constructive set of simulations that are more than "mere games." This group includes aircraft flight simulators, battle tactics simulators, railroad dispatcher simulators, etc., and are another use for your //c. That they have serious value is best illustrated by the fact that one friend of the authors, who has developed some tactics-type games, was recently a guest in the Pentagon's training section because of his work. These simulations are valid teaching tools; just ask the MBA graduate who has sweated through a marketplace-simulation game in competition with his classmates.

One difficulty faced by //c owners is that, because of the exotic copy protection schemes used by some manufacturers, some games will not boot in the half-high disk drive. As noted earlier, the companies are modifying their new products to be usable by the //c, so make sure a game will work before you buy it.

The //c will play games as well as any //e, and uses the same types of peripherals, including color monitors, joy sticks, and paddles. Remember, the OPEN APPLE and SOLID APPLE keys flanking the SPACE bar on the keyboard are wired to operate just like the paddle pushbuttons.

We have now covered the most-used functions for Apple //c's; they are enough to make the personal computer a valuable aid to everyday life. In the next chapter, we'll look at some more intensive activities that you may want to try.

6

Advanced Functions and BASIC

Programming Languages

Many people who buy Apple //c computers will never go beyond using the four applications described in the previous chapter. This means they'll be missing many of the fascinating things that the //c can do. What we'd like to do in this chapter is to tell you about some of the more advanced things you can do with an Apple //c.

First, we will be going into some detail on the //c version of the BASIC programming language, but since a full excursion into BASIC would require another book, all we'll be able to do is whet your appetite. After you've been introduced to BASIC we'll take a look at the //c's ability to produce graphic images, followed by a look at Pascal, and finally, machine language.

The computer does not know how to do anything "by itself." It must be instructed (told what to do). This is done through various programming languages. The native language of the computer is actually a series of electrical pulses, which can be understood by humans but understanding them requires a great deal of concentration. To understand these pulses you need some means of detecting them such as flashing lights which correspond to the pulses as they occur. Since understanding the native language of computers is difficult to learn to do, other programming languages have been developed. These programming languages closely resemble English (or some other spoken language) and are classed as "higher-level" languages. That is, they are more nearly like our language(s) and more unlike the computer's native language. Since high-level languages are understandable to us, but are not understandable to the computer, an "interpreter" or "compiler" is used to change the high-level language that we understand (with a little bit of effort) into one which the computer understands.

One of the most-used high level programming languages, and the one that is built into the //c, is BASIC. BASIC is an acronym for "Beginner's All-purpose Symbolic Instruction Code." BASIC was developed at Dartmouth University so that students could quickly learn to program the University's large computer system in order to do much of their scientific and mathematical work. Over the years many "dialects" of BASIC have been written. Each new microcomputer has a version of BASIC written for it. (Scratch a Computer Science professor, and you get *his or her* ideal computer language; the current climate does not foster uniformity.) The dialect of BASIC in the //c is called Applesoft.

Commands

There are over 45 commands in Applesoft BASIC. We will not cover all of these in detail, but we will introduce you to some of the more useful ones. This should be enough to get you started with programming. Probably the easiest command to understand is PRINT. The PRINT command causes characters to display on the screen so that you can see what is happening. PRINT is the way to tell the computer to "show me this." PRINT in Applesoft BASIC has two main functions: in one mode it displays the result of calculations, similar to a calculator; in the other it simply duplicates what it reads after the PRINT command.

If you type **PRINT 2 + 3** and then press the «RETURN» key, the computer will dutifully respond with a 5 on the screen. Remember that on the //c you may type the command as "print" (lower-case) or "PRINT" (upper-case);

> **PRINT 2 + 3**
> or
> print 2 + 3

and the computer will respond correctly to either format. You can program in either the 40 column or the 80 column format. Just as it responds to either upper- or lower-case command entries, your //c isn't particular about the column format you select.

Incidentally, throughout this discussion of programming you will see notation like «RETURN». That is a standard means of indicating that you are to press the key indicated between the brackets when such an instruction is shown. «RETURN» therefore means "Press the Return key."

Modes   There are two "modes" in which the computer "understands" BASIC: *immediate* and *deferred*. The *immediate* mode requires no line number preceding the command(s) and any command issued is executed immediately after you press «RETURN». (Clever naming, eh what?!) The example shown above are in the immediate mode and use the "calculator" style of display.

In the *deferred* mode, each line of a program must have a number, and the computer will store the commands away in its memory until the RUN command is typed and the «RETURN» key is pressed. Once you have typed RUN and pressed «RETURN», the computer will begin to execute each line in numerical order. Sometimes, after you press «RETURN», you don't see anything on the screen for a brief amount of time. When this happens, the computer has taken a moment to perform a calculation. If your computer encounters a line in your program that contains PRINT, something will be displayed on the screen.

When using the Apple screen for programming you will be able to display 24 lines of code. If they were numbered, which they aren't, you would see the numbers from 1 to 24. It might seem foolish for us to point this out, but some applications, such as graphics, actually use a zero value (see graphics discussion in the next chapter) as a beginning line number.

Since you only have room for 24 lines of program code, you may run out of screen space before you finish entering, changing, and testing your code. Pretty soon the screen is so full of characters that you can't really tell what's what. In order to eliminate some of the confusion, Applesoft BASIC includes a command for clearing the screen (don't worry, the computer won't forget what you have already typed if you use this command).

Home

The Applesoft command to clear the screen and reposition the cursor at the upper left corner is HOME. This command will work in either the *immediate* or the *deferred* mode. If your machine isn't on, turn it on. If it is, and you have been typing in practice lines of code, type HOME and press «RETURN» so you can start with a clean screen. Now that you know how to clear the screen, try some samples of the PRINT command that use the //c as a calulator:

Example	Command	Result
1.	PRINT 2 + 3	5
2.	PRINT 2 + (3 * 4)	14
3.	PRINT (2 + 3) * 4	20
4.	PRINT 2 * (3 ^ 3)	54
5.	PRINT 2 ^ 3 + 3	11
6.	PRINT 2 ^ (3 + 3)	64

If you look carefully at the print statements you will notice that the result of the statement changes with the location of the parentheses even when the same operators are used. This is known as precedence in arithmetic operations. Precedence means that the computer has software that tells it which operations are "most important", and it performs them in the assigned order of precedence. The first operation Applesoft calculates is any operation located inside parentheses. Whatever value is reached by computing the equation inside a set of parentheses will subsequently be used in further calculations. If there are parentheses inside of parentheses, the computer calculates the innermost equation and then uses the determined value with the equated value in the next set.

It is important that the numbers of left- and right-parentheses are matched. You must have just as many left parentheses as you have right parentheses. The following example shows how the computer deals with nested parentheses (parentheses inside of parentheses.)

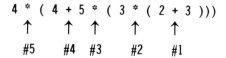

First, the 2 and 3 are added (5). Then the five is multiplied by 3 (15). The 15 is multiplied by 5 (75), four is added to that (79), and finally the 79 is multiplied by 4 to give the final result of 316.

Precedence & Parentheses

Although the numbers and operators in examples 2 and 3 of the PRINT statements above are in the same order, the parentheses change which operation is done first. In 2 the 3 and 4 are multiplied and the product added to the 2; in 3 the 2 and 3 are added together and the sum multiplied by the 4. As you can see, the simple placement of the parentheses can have dramatic effect on your calculations. Exponential operations follow the parentehses in importance. They are indicated by the caret (>) sign. It can be found on top of the "6" key on your //c keyboard. In 5 of our examples, 2 is raised to the third power. This result is then added to the remaining 3 in the equation. In example 6, the addition is done first because it is inside the parentheses. Remember, parentheses have precedence. After performing the addition the 2 is raised to the 6th power yielding the answer of 64.

Next in order of precedence are multiplication and division which are done left to right in the order shown, barring parentheses of course. Some versions of BASIC on other machines have division taking precedence over multiplication. However, in Applesoft BASIC, division and multiplication have equal precedence. In example 7 below, 2 is multiplied by 5 yielding 10. The 10 is then divided by 4, giving the final result of 2.5.

Example	Command	Result
7.	2 * 5 / 4	2.5
8.	2 / 5 * 4	1.6
9.	2 / (5 * 4)	.05

Finally, addition and subtraction operations are performed, again in the order in which they appear on the program line. Remember, we got into this trying to show that the PRINT command may be used to tell the computer that it should perform a series of calculations and display the result. Simple commands such as PRINT do not require you to SAVE the program and then RUN it in order to see the result. Now let's use the PRINT command to put the //c into a typewriter mode.

Using Quotation Marks

When using the PRINT command to display information other than the result of calculations, the characters that you want displayed must be included between a double quotation mark (") -- notice that this (") is really the double quote and not two single quotation marks or two apostrophes. This is achieved by pressing «SHIFT» and the punctuation key at the same time. Actually, only the opening quote is required when using Applesoft unless you want to include more on your program line. In that case, you must use the second quote to separate the text (or characters) to be printed from any additional instructions. In the first case you would use:

10.   PRINT "Hello, how are you?"

   is just the same to the computer as

11.   PRINT "Hello, how are you?

The second type of PRINT statement — the one we discussed that included additional instructions, is called a multiple statement line. A single line of code which contains several statements must have each statement separated by a colon (:); each new statement must start with an Applesoft instruction.

This second case would be:

Example   **Type**
12.   PRINT "Hello"

             Display will show: Hello

13.   PRINT "This is a #*@*! example."

             Display will show: This is a #*@*! example.

14.   PRINT "This is one":PRINT "This is two

             Display will show: This is one
                                  This is two

15.   `PRINT "This is one";:PRINT "This is two`

Display will show: `This is oneThis is two`

16.   `PRINT "This is one",:PRINT "This is two`

Display will show: `This is one This is two`

In 14 you see that each PRINT statement will produce its own line on the screen *unless* it is followed by a semicolon as in example 15 which shows what happens when the semicolon is used. The computer jargon for what happens when the semicolon is used is "suppression." The semicolon lets the computer know you want to continue printing on the same line. In example 16 you see that the comma will also "suppress the line feed" and it will move the second literal (anything inside the quote marks) to a new postion on the screen. Each such position is called a print zone. The semicolon in our example works somewhat like a TAB key found on a typewriter and the //c. When you press the «TAB» key the cursor moves to the right a predetermined number of spaces to a TAB "stop". TAB stops may be redefined and the print zone positions are fixed.

The TAB Statement

Using a comma limits you to placement of literals (the characters inside a double quote, remember?) Positions available are character locations 1, 17, 33, 49, and 65 along an 80-character line. Suppose you want to have your deathless prose appear at some other position along the line? To do this you will need to include a TAB statement (see example 17). You may set the TAB position at any character location up to 255. The format for using the TAB statement, which may only be used with the PRINT statement, is as follows:

Example   **Type**

17.   `PRINT TAB(23) "This is at 23"`

Display will show:`This is at 23`

(beginning at the 23rd character position from the left edge.)

The text display begins at position 23. You can even use several TAB statements in one PRINT statement, as in example 18.
The following line of code:

Example   **Type**
18.   `PRINT TAB(13)"This is 13"TAB(27)"This is 27"`

          Display will show: `This is 13`   `This is 27`

The two literals should now be displayed on the screen at their appropriate positions.

You can also use a TAB in a PRINT statement to print out results of calculations at desired locations. This is done without using quotation marks.

19.   `PRINT TAB(5)10/2TAB(85)51/3*5`

          Display will show: `5`
                             `85`

The 85 appears under the 5 because the line is only 80 characters long and the command requested position 85. This forced the computer to display the result in a position on the row below the first printed value. The computer counted out 80 characters and ran out of the room on the line. It continued counting on the next line down until it reached the desired 85. The one thing that you must remember is that you cannot TAB backwards. The following example would be illegal.

Example   **Type**
20.   `PRINT TAB(7)"THIS IS O.K."TAB(23)"AND SO IS`
               `THIS"TAB(17)"BUT THIS IS NOT`

What happens (did you try it?) is that the third phrase will print immediately after the second -- no intervening space.

         `THIS IS O.K.`   `AND SO IS THISBUT THIS IS NOT`

This same type of crowding will occur if you type several literals on the same line, enclose each in its own set of quotation marks but omit punctuation (comma or semicolon), as in the following example.

Example **Type**
21. PRINT "THIS IS ONE""THIS IS TWO""THIS IS THREE"

Display will show:
THIS IS ONETHIS IS TWOTHIS IS THREE

If you try to type the three phrases of example 21 but forget to add quotes to the center literal, you will see the following result:

THIS IS ONE0THIS IS THREE

The computer printed what was inside the first set of quotes (THIS IS ONE),but when it encountered something with words not in quotes (THIS IS TWO), it found no delimiter (in this case the quotes) so it printed a zero. When it finds another literal, which it dutifully prints out (THIS IS THREE). Delimiters are marks which set apart different portions of commands so that the computer recognizes that a different action is required. Quotes, parentheses, and slash marks (/) are among the characters used as delimiters.

Control Characters

The //c also understands a set of special characters called control characters. They are called control characters because you must hold down the «Control» key (in the same manner that you use the Shift key) found at the left edge of the "home" row of keys, while you press some other alphanumeric key. While most of the Control characters are not very exciting — all they do is move the cursor to various places on the screen, or even appear to do nothing at all — they can be very important to programmers. However, one Control character is a real attention-getter. If you have been working on this late at night and figure that everyone else ought to be up enjoying the computer with you, try "printing" out the following:

Example   **Type**

22.   `PRINT CHR$(7)CHR$(7)CHR$(7)CHR$(7)`

Do you have bells ringing? Or maybe the better expression with the //c is "do you hear beeps?" If you didn't hear anything after you pressed «Return» it may be because the volume knob (just below the left edge of the keyboard) has been turned to its minimum position.

Using CHR$(7) tells the computer to do something which you could not do from the keyboard without using a Control sequence. CHR$(7) is the ASCII (American Standard Code for Information Interchange) code for Control-G. Control-G is also called "bell." This code was first applied to the teletype machine. On teletype machines, a real bell signalled the operator on the receiving end of a transmission that the message was completed. CHR$ may also be used with any other number in the ASCII code to generate one of the ASCII characters on that list. (See Appendix A.) Try the following with your //c and see what happens.

Example   **Type**

23.   `CHR$(32)`   (it's the space bar)

24.   `CHR$(65)`   A

25.   `CHR$(97)`   a

While there may not appear to be any need for you to use ASCII characters very often since the //c has an expanded keyboard, knowing about them may be helpful if you want to translate programs written for other machines so they will run on your //c.

We could continue working in the *immediate* mode but we wouldn't fully demonstrate the power of the computer. What makes a computer really powerful is its ability to store a set of instructions and execute them at a later time.

Writing Your Own Program

Since a program must be executed in a set sequence, each line of a program is assigned a number as the program is developed; the numbers are assigned so the computer can logically execute the program. They do not have to be typed into the machine in any particular order because the computer will execute them in the correct numerical order. Good programming practice dictates that you assign numbers in increments of no less than 10, since you will later think of at least 2 or 3 lines that must be inserted to improve the program. (If you number your program lines by increments of 1, there is no room to insert another line because the computer does not recognize fractional line numbers such as "13.4.").

Let's rewrite some of our previous examples as lines in an Applesoft program. After you rewrite them you can execute them. What you will be doing is writing an actual computer program and then running it. Begin by typing in the following:

Example Number	Program line to type
4a.	10 PRINT 2 + (3 ^ 3)
5a.	20 PRINT 2 ^ 3 + 3
6a.	30 PRINT 2 ^ (3 + 3)

You will notice that by starting each line of code with a line number, the only thing that happens when you complete a line by pressing «RETURN» is that the cursor moves to the next line on the screen. In the immediate mode, pressing «Return» caused something to happen. Adding line numbers tells the computer that you want to create many lines of code before you make anything happen. Each time you press «Return» the computer has stored the program line in its memory, where it can be found later when the execute command (RUN) is issued.

Now that you have all three lines typed, type one more line:

```
5 HOME
```

Remember, because we numbered by tens, it is possible to insert this new line of code by using line number 5. This is important because we need to include a HOME command in our program.

Now type

```
RUN <RETURN>
```

Did you get a clean screen with 54, 11, and 64 displayed at the lefthand side on the three top lines? You should have!

Screen Display
Let's take a look at how we might use some simple programming to display a full screen of information at one time without crowding. You might want to include the following: a title, centered a few lines down from the top, the program author's name in the lower right corner, and the date of the program in the lower left corner. Further, let's use some ingenuity and highlight the title. Computer programs are more often known by the title than by the author's name. Since you want the reader to be aware of the author's name (you *are* important, after all!), have the name appear on the screen for a brief time before the date appears. The reader can then concentrate on one thing at a time — title first, then author's

name, then date — instead of reading the entire screen
at one time. How are you going to get the program to do
all of this in the sequence you want? Most of the
positioning we want can be accomplished using two
additional screen placement commands, HTAB and
VTAB, standing for horizontal tab and vertical tab.

These commands use "arguments". Using arguments
is a way of setting values for the command. In this case,
the argument is a number, which comes after the command on the program line. VTAB can have an argument
from 1 to 24; HTAB, an argument from 1 to 255,
although it is probably most useful to limit the horizontal argument to either 40 or 80, depending upon the
screen display mode you are using. Incidentally, an
argument in this case is not something to be avoided in
the interests of peace; in fact, an argument is essential
for these two statements. Here is the screen we wish to
display:

```
The Great Computer Mystery




          Copyright 1984
               by
          Bogden Trashe
```

Before we can use the HTAB and VTAB statements to center the title on the screen, we must first determine where our text should begin for it to be centered. First, we must count the number of characters in the title (including spaces), then subtract that number from the total available on one line (40 in our example) and, finally, divide by 2. This will put our first character in horizontal positon 7 of our forty column display.

"The Great Computer Mystery" contains 26 characters, so the math looks like this:

```
40 - 26 = 14; 14 / 2 = 7
```

That makes the program line to print the title look like:

```
50  VTAB 3: HTAB 7: PRINT "The Great Computer
    Mystery"
```

This number is the result of our division. This is for line 3 on the screen.

The other lines on the screen could be obtained as follows:

```
60  VTAB 22: HTAB 25: PRINT "By"
70  VTAB 23: HTAB 25: PRINT ""Bogden Trashe''
80  VTAB 21: PRINT ""Copyright 1984''
```

Notice that line 80 does not contain an HTAB statement; without one, the computer will print the literal in horizontal position 1, the left margin. We still need to clear the screen for our wonderful display, so add:

```
10  HOME
```

If you want to see your program before you run it, type LIST «RETURN». You will see that the computer has placed line 10 in its proper position, even though you didn't type it until after line 80 was saved in memory.

Remember, we discussed this earlier. Now if you RUN the program, you will see the various lines of the display in the locations you selected; if you watch very closely you will also see that they appeared in the order you specified. There is a way to slow down the printing to the screen so that it is easier to see the correct order of display. Try typing

```
SPEED = 150 <RETURN>
```

and then type RUN again. You will see the letters coming up one at a time. The SPEED command can be used from within a program as well as in the *immediate* mode. Display speed can be set from 0 (slowest) to 255 (normal speed.) Once you have invoked a slower display SPEED, the computer will continue to use this for all your display commands until you return to the default value (normal speed) by typing

```
SPEED = 255 <RETURN>
```

The title still isn't highlighted (sob-sob!) Oh well, that's easy to fix!

```
40 INVERSE
50 VTAB 3: HTAB 7: PRINT "The Great Computer Mystery"
```

Now type RUN again. Ooopps! Everything is highlighted — and that's not all; you should have some very strange-looking characters in the author's name and the copyright. Now what? Like SPEED, INVERSE is a command that will remain in effect until cancelled. How? UNINVERSE? Not exactly, the opposite of INVERSE is NORMAL. So insert the following line:

```
55 NORMAL
```

RUN the program again. Now it should be right!

The change in the title is easy to understand, but where did those weird characters come from when the lower case letters were put into inverse? Well, it has to do with the way the Apple ROM monitor programs tell the computer which character to display on the screen. There are 128 different characters available with the ordinary ASCII code. Since Apple added two other modes and their corresponding characters to the //c, the normal display would require 384 different codes to handle them all. Unfortunately, 256 is the maximum number of different character codes you can have with the current microprocessor in the Apple II family of machines. To accomodate this limitation, Apple sacrificed the lower-case letters in the inverse and flashing modes on the //c.

Flashing mode? FLASH is another command that will draw attention to information on the screen. But it can be annoying, especially if the display remains flashing on the screen for more than a few seconds. Suppose that you wanted to really draw attention to the title. You could write line 40 as:

```
40 FLASH
```

Try this modification and run your short program again. Everything is in the same as before except now the title is flashing. The title will continue to FLASH until you clear the screen. If you change the program (by adding a later line with HOME in it) you will eliminate the flash, but HOME will also eliminate all the other information on the screen when it is executed. To benefit from FLASH without losing your screen, or your sanity, you might try the addition of the next three lines:

```
 90 FOR I = 1 TO 500: NEXT I
100 INVERSE
110 VTAB 3: HTAB 7: PRINT "THE GREAT COMPUTER
MYSTERY"
```

RUN the program again; you will see that the title is eventually returned to its non-flashing inverse display. But what did line 90 do? The instructions in line 90 are called a delay loop. Looping is one way of getting the computer to take some time out to count (or do something else), before going on to the next line. In this instance, you told the computer to stop what it was doing until it had counted to 500. Since the computer is very fast at counting, and lots of other things too, it counted to 500 and then executed line 100, all in less than a second.

Another Advanced Display Technique

You remember that when we wanted to have the title centered, we did it by figuring out ourselves where the title should start. A better way to center *any* collection of characters (called a "string") requires learning about "variables" and "subroutines." It should be (almost) painless!

Think of a variable as a location in the computer's memory. Different values we are creating with our program are stored there. Sort of like a box at the post office, which can contain different letters and/or bills on different days of the month. There are two types of variables that can be used: a "numeric" variable, which obviously holds numerical data, and a second type known as a "string" variable. The string-variable "box" is designed to hold titles, words, combinations of letters, numbers, and other special characters. String variables are labeled with one or two letters, followed by the dollar sign; e.g., AP$, N$, TT$, etc. Having given the box a label, the computer can then find it anytime you ask for the contents of that particular box.

A numeric variable is a number (for example, 100) that the computer can use to calculate other values. A string variable is a group of characters. In a string variable, the numerals in the number 100 would look the same on the screen as they do when displayed as the numeric variable 100, but are not treated in the same manner by the computer. The computer cannot use the string variable 100 in any sort of calculation; it can only display it, as is, on the screen.

A "subroutine" is a short (usually), reusable section of programming code that performs a repetitive function. Subroutines are helpful because they prevent you from having to write the same code over and over. You write the code once and then tell the computer to go to the memory location for that code each time you need it. Each sub-routine should end with a command to return to the program where it left off. Once it returns it can proceed with the rest of the program.

Let's modify our title screen program. We will now let the computer calculate the proper spacing for centering and insert some variables and subroutines which should help you understand what we have been talking about. Begin by changing line 50 to read:

```
50 VTAB 3: TT$ = "THE GREAT COMPUTER MYSTERY"
```

and change line 100 to read:

```
VTAB 3: GOSUB 200
```

and add line 52.

```
52 GOSUB 200
```

Finally, at line 200 you will write your short subroutine:

```
200 HTAB ( (40 - LEN (TT$) / 2 ): PRINT TT$
210 RETURN
```

The LEN statement stands for Length and will count the number of characters in whatever literal is stored in the string variable TT$. As our title has 26 characters in it, LEN (TT$) is treated as a numeric variable with the value of 26.

Just to make sure that everything is correct, LIST your program as it now resides in memory. (Just type LIST «RETURN», remember?) It should look like this:

```
 10  HOME
 40  FLASH
 50  VTAB 3: TT$ = "THE GREAT COMPUTER MYSTERY"
 52  GOSUB 200
 55  NORMAL
 60  VTAB 22: HTAB 25: PRINT "By"
 70  VTAB 23: HTAB 25: PRINT "Bogden Trashe"
 80  VTAB 21: PRINT "Copyright 1984"
 90  FOR I = 1 TO 500: NEXT I
100  INVERSE
110  VTAB 3: GOSUB 200
200  HTAB ( (40 – LEN (TT$) / 2 ): PRINT TT$
210  RETURN
```

To prevent a problem when you RUN your program, insert one last line,

```
199 END
```

and RUN it. Works, doesn't it? A program with a subroutine needs the END command (line 199) to keep it from "crashing" — that most undesirable of computer catastrophes. The END command does just what you'd think: causes the computer to end all further action on the program in memory. If it were not there, after executing line 110, the computer would go to the next line in order (200) and then proceed to 210, where it would encounter the command, RETURN. Since you had not arrived at this level of the program by use of the GOSUB command, the computer would generate the message RETURN WITHOUT GOSUB, beep at you in a very unfriendly manner, and cease any further cooperation.

You have now been introduced to the art of computer programming. There is much more to learn, if you are interested. Remember, you'll have to think logically and do a lot of "puzzle solving" to make longer and more complex programs work.

7

Beyond BASIC; Graphics and other Languages

Graphics   There are three modes for graphic display on the //c: *low resolution* ("Lo-Res"), *high resolution* ("Hi-Res"), and *double high-resolution* ("Double Hi-Res"). You might make "pictures" using the keyboard to type in various symbols, but the graphics modes were designed so that you could create pictures using lines and blocks. In addition to straight lines and blocks, the *high resolution* modes also allow you to draw curved figures such as arcs, circles and conic sections. The size of the blocks in the *low resolution* mode limits you to a very rough approximation of a circular shape on the screen.

Even though Lo-Res may seem somewhat crude, it allows us to present an understandable introduction to Apple's graphics capabilities. For that reason, we will concentrate on it in this chapter. Hi-Res and Double Hi-Res are similar to Lo-Res, but are much more complicated to learn.

Sixteen colors are available in Lo-Res. We assume at you'll use a color monitor or color TV set with your //c for the next few examples, but a "shades of gray" approximation will let you see what's happening even on a monochrome monitor.

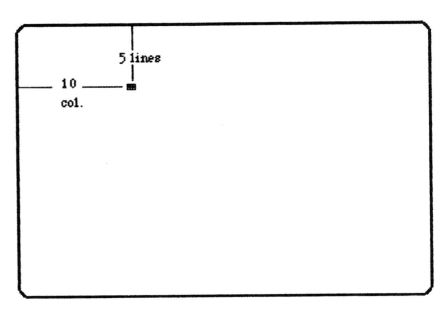

Lo-Res PLOT 10,5

Low-resolution Graphics Colors

Decimal	Hex	Name
0	0	Black
1	1	Magenta
2	2	Dark Blue
3	3	Purple
4	4	Dark Green
5	5	Grey 1
6	6	Medium Blue
7	7	Light Blue
8	8	Brown
9	9	Orange
10	A	Grey 2
11	B	Pink
12	C	Light Green
13	D	Yellow
14	E	Aquamarine
15	F	White

The graphics commands are extensions of Applesoft BASIC, and the programs are in that language. To enter the Lo-Res graphics mode, type GR «RETURN». The top 20 lines of text screen now become a graphics screen. In this graphics mode, the screen is divided into 1600 blocks. Each of these blocks is as wide as a text character, and half as high. In 20 lines and 40 characters, then, the blocks form a 40 x 40 grid. Only the bottom four screen lines will be available for you to read what you have typed in from the keyboard. If you are currently working on a program, the screen will remain in the *text* mode until you RUN the program. To return to the *text* mode after writing and running a Lo-Res program, type TEXT «RETURN». This command restores the screen to the *text* mode and lets you see your program listing.

Let's try some of the Lo-Res command statements in the *immediate* mode. (If you do not remember what the *immediate* mode is, go back to Chapter Six and refresh your memory.) Type GR and then type:

```
COLOR = 9 <RETURN>
PLOT 10,5 <RETURN>
```

The first line changes the color from black to orange. On the //c, nine is the code number for orange. If you are using a monochrome monitor the cursor will appear as a four by four set of small dots in a block (if you look *very* closely!). You should be able to see that the block is located one-quarter of the way from the left side of the screen, and one-eighth of the way from the top of the screen.

If you are interested in seeing the appearance of the other colors available on the //c, type in the following small BASIC program and RUN it. You can run this program on a monochrome monitor, but the display will not be in color. (Rather than continuing to write out «RETURN», we're going to assume that you'll press «RETURN» after each line from here on.)

```
10 GR
20 FOR P = 0 TO 15
30 COLOR = P
40 PLOT P*2, P*2
50 NEXT P
60 END
```

If you count the blocks on the screen after you type in and RUN this program, you may see only 15 blocks, not 16, as you would expect if our count were from 0 through 15, inclusive. If the screen you are using has a black background, the block made with COLOR = 0 (black) is there, but invisible. Does that give you some ideas about how to erase a graphics line on the screen? Yep... replace it with black.

Lines 20 through 50 of this sample program are actually a FOR... NEXT loop. FOR... NEXT loops allow the program to repeat the series of steps in program lines between FOR and NEXT a specified number of times. The number is specified in the FOR statement; a variable "P" will step up from zero to 15, so the loop will be travelled sixteen times. Each time the program completes a loop, it then checks to see if P, the loop counter, is larger than the upper limit of the FOR statement (15 in this case). If not, the program will increase P by one and repeat the loop. After 16 circuits, when P reaches 16, the program "drops out" of the loop and moves on, executing the first program line following the NEXT statement.

Line 30 sets the color code number equal to P, as well, so we have it doing double duty. Line 40 sets the block location on the screen; this location depends on the value of P for that trip through the loop or "iteration." With each iteration, we change both the color (line 30) and the location of the block (line 40).

Suppose you want to have a diagonal multi-color on the screen (it is actually a series of connected blocks).

Modify line 40 in the program to read:

```
40 PLOT P,P
```

and RUN the program again. Did it work? Of course! Since P is a variable that changes with each iteration of the loop, the program will plot 0,0, then 1,1, 2,2, and so forth through 15,15. The //c is an obedient servant, doing exactly what you tell it to. In *this* case it also did what you *wanted* it to. Now suppose you want to draw an "X" on the screen, using multiple colors. Delete line 60 (just type 60 «RETURN») and add the following lines to your program:

```
60 FOR Q = 0 TO 15
70 PLOT 15 – Q, Q
80 NEXT Q
90 END
```

When this one is RUN, you should have a multicolored X in the upper left quadrant of the screen. The arms may appear shorter in the upper left and upper right corners of your X because those squares are black.

How about an X which goes from corner to corner of the entire screen? Let's use a single color this time for each leg. Modify line 20 to read:

```
20 FOR P = 0 TO 39
```

and line 60 to read:
```
FOR Q = 0 TO 39
```

Modify line 30 so that COLOR = 9 and add line 55
```
55 COLOR = 4
```

Last, modify line 70 to read:
```
70 PLOT 39 – Q, Q
```

Now when the program is RUN you'll have an orange line from upper left to lower right and a green one from upper right to lower left. They will be drawn in a corresponding order with both lines starting from the top and going to the bottom of the screen.

Now let's design a program that uses motion. In order to make a line move, you will have to draw portions of it at one location, then draw it at a second location as it is deleted at the first location. If you form a line point and delete it right away, the picture will be too jerky to be seen. Because of this we have included line 55 to slow down the execution of the program.

We have also included Lines 10 and 50, which begin with the reserved word REM. In BASIC, any program line beginning with REM will be ignored by the computer when it's executing a program. The REM or Remark statement allows us to insert labels into a program for us humans to see. Use REM statements to remind yourself what an adjacent section of program code actually does.

```
10   REM construct wall
20   GR
30   COLOR = 2
40   FOR Y = 32 TO 39: PLOT 33,Y: PLOT 34,Y: NEXT
50   REM construct cannonball
55   SPEED = 150
60   FOR X = 0 TO 38: COLOR = 13: PLOT X,35: PLOT X +
     1,35:
     COLOR = 0: PLOT X,35: NEXT
70   PLOT 39,35
99   END
```

If you typed this program in and ran it you know what it does. If you were not sitting at your //c while you were reading this (and why weren't you?) you should know that this program builds a blue wall and pokes a hole in it with a yellow cannonball. Sounds interesting, huh? For those of you who did type the program in and run it, you may have noticed that making the top of the wall obey the laws of gravity is not easy. In fact, we feel it is so complex that it is a topic for a more detailed text on programming. If you do want to attempt it on your own you should plan a way to have the bricks above the line of the cannonball's path be re-plotted at lower and lower locations until they end up on the ground (graphics display line 39.)

As with movie animation, the illusion of motion is obtained through many revisions of the screen display, changing the colors of certain blocks with your program, a little at a time. The FOR . . . NEXT loop, which we have compressed into line 60 of our program, "moves" the cannonball one block-location at a time.

There is no conceptual difference between Apple Lo-Res and any other video graphics system. Each block is controlled individually, and corresponds to a specific location in the computer's memory. With Hi-Res graphics, the dots are much smaller than the Lo-Res blocks. That makes the plotting much more difficult.

There are many graphics software products on the market that allow you to create Hi-Res displays without having to descend to the time-consuming, bit-mapping, line-and-dot plots. A recent Apple release uses the power of your //c built-in electronics to best advantage; it's called MousePaint.

MousePaint

MousePaint is a graphics program that comes with the Apple Mouse. It does most (but not all) of what Mac-Paint will do on Apple's more expensive Macintosh computer. This form of graphic expression is available to you with no muss or fuss because the //c's 9-pin connector accepts a mouse as easily as it accepts a joystick.

Essentially, MousePaint turns the electronic mouse in your hand into an electronic painting tool. Just plug in the mouse, boot the MousePaint disk, and the screen becomes a canvas. Unlike the //e or other older Apple II models, you do not have to insert an auxilliary board into the //c to run MousePaint because all of the circuitry for the mouse is built in. In fact, you should buy the mouse only, not the package that includes the board. The first time you try MousePaint, it might be wise to go through Apple's charming instruction course on mousery. It's another of the excellent self-teaching courses Apple has prepared.

For easily creating graphics, the mouse is as good as it gets, folks. MousePaint lets you "paint" using brushes of various sizes and shapes, draw with a pencil, or, if you have a lot to cover, spray with a spray can. If you want to enter text into your graphics you can use the mouse to select five different letter styles. The mouse also lets you draw straight lines or geometric shapes. For the sloppy user, the mouse can be used to erase if you make a mistake. Remember, all of this (except typing the text letters) is done by moving and clicking the mouse. If you need more, the mouse and MousePaint let you draw geometric shapes automatically and fill them with your choice of 30 patterns. If you aren't satisfied with what you've done, you can use the Editor Box to move, flip, invert, cut, paste, or delete whatever you have drawn. For variety, you can vary line widths. MousePaint also allows you to edit the drawing by enlarging it. Each dot in the enlarged section suddenly looks like a Lo-Res block; they're called "Fatbits." You can add or delete one dot at a time.

While using MousePaint you only see only a portion of the workspace. To bring different segments into view you use a small "grabbing hand" to reposition the entire worksheet. Once a picture or document is set up the way you want it, you can save the picture as a disk file. To do this, you might need to refer to the previously discussed rules for ProDOS. Remember, you must save the picture or document using a pathname with the names of both

the disk volume and your picture, e.g. /PIX/SAMPLE.
You can't directly select a disk drive.

**Non-Resident
Languages**

Your Apple //c also uses computer languages besides
Applesoft BASIC, but only Applesoft BASIC resides in
the computer's ROM. To use other programming
languages, you will need to purchase additional program
disks to load these non-resident languages into the computer. Apple's Pascal and Logo, for example, come with
disks and manuals as a package. Both Pascal and Logo
are considered to be excellent languages for teaching
and learning.

Logo, while most closely associated with teaching
small children to learn about computers, is by no means
only for kids. Two Logo packages are currently available: Apple's enhanced Logo, and the MIT version from
Krell Software. To learn Logo, you are shown how to
move an imaginary "turtle" on the screen. The turtle has
a pen tied to his tail. As you move the turtle, he leaves a
trail, or colored line. So if you enter a command telling
the turtle to go RIGHT 50 spaces, you'll know you were
right if the screen image looks as if he did so. There's
more to Logo than turtles, but that's the most familiar
beginning point to learn the language.

Pascal, a "high-level" language, is considerably more
powerful than BASIC or Logo. Pascal has become the
language of choice for many serious programmers
because it uses a structured approach to programming.
Unlike BASIC, it makes life much more difficult for a
programmer who would prefer to program in a sloppy
fashion. The payoff for using Pascal's structured
approach over BASIC's relatively free-form one, is
speed. Pascal programs execute faster than comparable
BASIC programs.

No programming language is capable of being learned
in one evening, despite the claims of some manufacturers
and some writers. Your competence will be a direct

result of the effort you invest. Sorry, but that's the way it is. Another fact about programming is that some people are just better at it than others because they've usually worked harder or longer at it. Having said that, let us also add that the largest obstacle standing in the way of your learning to program a computer is the belief that only mutants can do it, not ordinary people. (Comments on the appearance of some computer wizards are not welcome at this time!)

So which language is easiest to learn? Which is easiest to start with? We come to yet another eternal verity: Different people prefer different languages. You'll find your favorite and swear by it, and other programmers will think you are mad. Practically speaking, the Apple //c's Applesoft BASIC is probably the best place to start learning programming, largely because it is included in the machine. If you have gone through the BASIC and Lo-Res exercises in this book, you already have been programming in Applesoft.

The Machine's Language

A program written in one of the higher-level languages must be "translated" for the computer into its own language before the program's instructions are useful to the machine. The computer uses the natural on-off state of electrical impulses to count, using a number system compatible with the on and off pulses. This system is called binary arithmetic, and uses only two distinct symbols, 0 and 1. 0 represents "off", and 1 represents "on". The binary number system uses base 2, just as decimal numbers use base 10. Hexadecimal numbers use base 16.

The only reasons why we're used to base 10 can be counted on the fingers of two hands. In fact, the reasons *are* the fingers on your two hands. If humans had sixteen fingers, we would use base 16. The ASCII table in Appendix A shows equivalent numbers for the binary, decimal, and hexadecimal systems; here's a smaller comparison table to show the differences:

Comparison of Numbers

Decimal	Binary	Hexadecimal
1	1	1
2	10	2
3	11	3
4	100	4
5	101	5
6	110	6
7	111	7
8	1000	8
9	1001	9
10	1010	A
11	1011	B
12	1100	C
13	1101	D
14	1110	E
15	1111	F
16	1120	10

Table 7-1

So the number of items some people consider as unlucky is "1101" in base 2 and "D" in base 16. In base 16, there are 32 states in the Union. Notice that the squares of the base always add a digit; 10, 100, 1000, 10000 are universal, regardless of the base. Hexadecimal, by the way, uses the letters A through F to make up the symbols that the decimal system doesn't need.

To express a perfectly reasonable decimal number like 198 in binary requires eight digits (11000110). If all programmers had to write using only binary numbers, there would be very few people doing programming at all. Not only would you have to remember what the patterns of 1's and 0's were, but you would also have to remember which instruction was represented by the number codes.

But machine language is the champion as far as execution speed is concerned. Machine language is less like human language than any of the other programming languages. Because it is less like human speech, the computer does not need to have programming instructions interpreted before it can execute them. Machine language directly addresses the functions programmed into the 65C02 microchip, telling it, for example, to take a number from a certain memory location, do something to it, and put it in the same or another memory location.

To make things a little easier for the programmer without losing the advantage of execution speed, which is found in machine language, an intermediate language exists called Assembly language. There are two- or three-letter mnemonics for the different functions, and the number system used is called hexadecimal, or a base-16 number system. The same number (198) which required 8 digits in binary requires only two digits in hexadecimal ($C6). Besides, hexadecimal is very easy to translate into binary. We use the dollar sign to indicate a hexadecimal number, by the way. Is this getting complicated? Well, that's why the BASIC and Pascal languages were invented. But hang on for a few more moments.

We're going to take a small excursion into the depths of the Apple //c (unsuccessfully resisting the temptation to say we're going to the Apple's core). First, we'll do something in BASIC and then repeat it in the machine's native tongue. For our example, let's place a character on the screen.

Remember, each location on the screen is governed by a location in the computer's memory. In BASIC, we PEEK to see what value is in a given memory location, and we POKE to place a value between 0 and 255 (decimal) in a memory location. When we POKE a value into a memory location that controls the screen display, the ASCII character corresponding to that value will appear on the screen. Try entering this in the *immediate* mode:

```
HOME
POKE 1082,129
```

These are decimal numbers. 1082 is the number of a memory location (think of a bank of post office boxes), and 129 is the ASCII code number for the capital "A." So, a capital *A* should appear on the screen in a space that had formerly been blank. If you POKE 1083,130, you'll place a *B* into the "box" next to the *A*. The screen display is not completely sequential in memory. If you want to learn all of the screen locations, your Reference Manual shows the layout.

BASIC doesn't really allow us to place a value directly into memory, and the POKE command is not really part of BASIC. It is an extension created for Apples by the helpful Mr. Wozniak to allow us to use "brute force" to place data into memory. Normally, BASIC values must be translated first.

Using machine language we can place the value directly in memory. The //c's Monitor instruction set for machine language uses hexadecimal ("Hex") arithmetic. Our BASIC POKEs were in decimal so they need to be translated, which we've done. First, type:

`CALL -151`

The number 151 is the memory address of the Monitor program in the Apple. Instead of the normal Applesoft prompt character ( ]), you'll see an asterisk prompt on the screen. You are now as far into the computer's cir-cuitry as any human can get without a soldering iron. Now type:

`43A : 82`

The letter *A* that we had on the screen because of our BASIC POKE, should have changed to a *B*. Typing 43A in Hex is the same as typing 1082 in decimal. The num-ber 82 Hex is the same as 130 decimal and, if you remember, 130 decimal is equal to the ASCII character *B*.

So $81 is *A* and $82 is *B*. You can go ahead and change the letter to a *C* now. Type `43A:83`. You get the idea. Now type `3D0G` <RETURN> (that's zero, not the letter "O") to return to BASIC. There's Applesoft's right brack-et prompt character again.

That's as far as we're going into machine language in this volume. It may be more than you wanted to know, but at least you have seen the Monitor and have returned in good health. If you really want to learn more about machine language, the //c Reference Manual has more on the Monitor commands, and there are many books on the subject. The best way to learn is in a class or by attending a user group session, which will teach this type of programming by using a Machine Language Assembler program.

So far, we have looked at the internals of the //c. Next on our agenda is the all-important, but sometimes frustrating, process of using your computer to communicate with the outside world.

8

Printing and Communicating

Transferring Information

The power of your //c increases when you connect it to external devices. Such connections are made to move information into or out of the computer. You may want that information to go two feet to a printer, fifty feet to another computer in the same building, or thousands of miles through a telephone line. Although most people think of computer communication as talking to other personal computers, large mainframe computers, or information network services, many of us begin communicating by "talking" to printers.

At first glance, it may seem an unlikely combination to consider printers and telecommunications devices in the same breath. The closer look which we'll take in this chapter shows, however, that both types of communication have almost the same characteristics. In both, what you're doing is transferring information, one letter or number at a time, through a wire connecting the computer to another device. Since data transmission is done at relatively high speeds, the possibilities for errors are quite high. One small electronic hiccup during the transmission and you can end up with skohg yud u4sq8k mrkgee.

One of the greatest sources of frustration for computer users, be they novice or expert, comes from trying to connect, or "interface," the computer to another machine, such as a printer. This becomes a greater problem when the machines come from different manufacturers who use different types of connections and instructions. Like the forward pass in football, three things can happen and two of them are bad:

(1) The data is transmitted properly;
(2) The data is transmitted, but garbled; or
(3) The data is not transmitted at all.

There are many links in the communications chain, and there are many possible things that can go wrong. Every one of the links must be correct in order for the process to work. When a printer just sits there instead of printing your term paper or letter, the problem could be one or more of the following:

(a) No power to the printer or computer
(b) Poor connection of the cable
(c) A broken or disconnected wire *in* the cable
(d) Malfunction in the computer output circuitry
(e) Malfunction in the printer circuitry
(f) Wrong switch settings for data in the printer or computer
(g) Wrong commands coming from the computer (software)
(h) Different settings for the data-transmission rate
(i) Different "protocol" or recognition signals expected

When problems occur, some manufacturers of hardware and software may respond to your request for help by telling you that they think the problem is in a part of the system that they did not manufacture. That's called finger-pointing. When that happens, it's not hard to see why people take up knitting, or why some personal computers gather dust.

Communicating between your //c and a printer or other device is not all trouble and strife, however. Once you do get your own system connected and operating, there is very little that can go wrong unless you disconnect or change something. A new piece of software may have to be configured to your system when you first use it, but thereafter it shouldn't be a problem.

Many of you will use only a few peripheral devices, such as a printer, a modem, or a plotter, so you really only need to know how to make a few connection arrangements. There's no reason why you have to know how to hook your system to everything. Therefore, this book will not dwell extensively on stop bits, odd and even parity, full and half duplex, Bell System standards, etc.. There are a few fundamental things to learn, but you don't need to drown in electronic or telephone theory.

Your //c has the most simple kind of hookup of any computer. To make things even easier, the ports on the back are marked with pictorial icons or symbols to help show you where the connections should be made. As we said, you're probably only interested in hooking up a few simple devices, which is not an impossible task, and won't require months of research. Each peripheral comes with its own manual. The line of peripherals manufactured by Apple is marketed with a series of interface kits that contain the appropriate cables for hooking an item to the //c. Follow the manuals and your connections should be trouble-free more than 95 per cent of the time.

If you are having trouble connecting your //c to any peripheral devices, the best solution is to have your dealer set up the connection in the store with equipment and software identical to yours, and verify that it works. Take notes, and set yours up the same way. Apple is spending a great deal of money on dealer information and training, and expects first-class performance. You should expect the same. Another source of direct help is the Apple User Group in your area; these groups are described in Chapter 9.

RS-232

Your Apple //c communicates with printers and modems through the two 5-pin serial ports on the back of the computer. It does this through cables that are connected to other devices. The //c uses RS-232 serial communications, the most commonly used serial interface standard. You won't find a parallel mode communication connection or capability on your //c. Many popular printers only use parallel connectors. Be sure that any printer or other peripheral you expect to use with the //c is equipped for RS-232 serial communication.

Most RS-232 serial devices are connected using "DB-25" D-type plugs and sockets with 25 possible pins. Since only five of those pins are actually needed for effective serial transmission, the //c designers used a 5-pin connector to save space and to be able to fit two ports on the machine. But, since most of the printers, plotters, modems, and other devices you'll want to hook to your //c use the 25-pin connector, your first step is to purchase a cable that has a 5-pin plug on one end, and a 25-pin plug or socket on the other. Apple dealers have these cables, either as separate items or as part of an interface kit. Whether the other end of a particular cable should have a 25-pin plug or a socket depends on what fixture is built into the other device. If you need them, plug-to-plug and socket-to-socket adapters are available. These items are not always included with the various devices, so you will need to verify, with your dealer, that the peripheral device you are buying will actually work with the //c that you have.

Since the software you purchase controls communications between your computer and its peripherals, it is possible that the connection will work perfectly with one or more of your software packages, and not work at all with another. As we noted, many programs will have to be "configured" for your printer, which means that you'll have to tell the program what special characters your printer uses as recognition signals.

Baud Rate

How fast can your data bits march through that cable to an external device? The old teletypes transmitted data at 110 bits per second. With seven bits per character, that's almost 16 letters per second. Personal computers generally use a 300-bit per second rate. The number of bits per second is known as the "baud" rate; data moving at 300 bits per second is said to be travelling at 300 baud. Lately, 1200 baud is becoming more common. (One "in" bumper sticker around computer folks is "Ma Bell Runs a Baudy House.")

A 9600 baud rate can also be used (that's almost 1400 characters per second, which will keep up with the capability of most printers) for transmitting data between computers. A speed of 9600 baud is most often used to communicate between computers and other devices in the same building, because the standard telephone system is not sensitive enough to hear the bits clearly at that speed (it cannot "maintain the data integrity").

The baud rate must be set the same for the devices on both ends of the line for the communication to be successful. Back to the football analogy: if the receiver is running too fast or too slow, the pass will be incomplete. Most printers and other devices have from 4 to 16 small switches that control the baud rate setup and other protocols. The manuals that come with the computer and printer should show how to set up the connection. But some hardware manuals are often unclear or too technical, and you need to be aware that they may not explain the whole story. As usual, make sure that the printer you buy will, in fact, work with your //c.

Protocols

The protocols, or recognition signals, used by computers tell them whether or not information that has been sent has also been correctly received. We're going to bypass the technical description of parity, stop bits, full and half duplex, and describe it another way. The following dialogue shows how full protocol verification works:

> Machine A: "Ready?"
> Machine B: "Yes."
> Machine A: "Here's the data."
> Machine B: "I have it."
> Machine A: "Read that back to me."
> Machine B: "Here it is."
> Machine A: "That's right" (or) "Nope, that's not what I sent. Here it is again. Ready?"

Signals continue until both devices agree on the data. The process goes by the incredibly technical term: — "handshaking."

Problems arise where there is no handshaking, which is the case with many printer connections. As we noted, either the printer just sits there dumbly (of course you made sure it was plugged in), or the printer prints gibberish. The combination of settings and commands that will make it work is in there somewhere. The most common source of error is the setting of the tiny rocker switches ("DIP switches") in many printers. First, follow the manual instructions. If the lashup still doesn't work, the best solution is to have your dealer or another person who has solved the problem show you the way.

Printers

Your printer will most likely be plugged into Serial Port 1 of your //c, which is the socket with the printer icon. With whatever printer you hook to your //c, you must make sure you have a serial interface printer (RS-232), not parallel. You must also make sure that all of the links in the communications chain are functioning. That chain begins with the software directing output to the socket where the printer is plugged and ends with everything on the paper that should be there, and nothing on the paper that shouldn't be. Don't let anyone tell you that there's "no way" to get it right, or that you'll have to "live with" funny marks on the sides, etc..

The printers most often hooked to personal computers are "impact" printers, so called because a metal or plastic device hits the paper through an inked ribbon, just like a typewriter. Impact printers come in two types; "dot-matrix" and "daisy wheel." Each type has its own advantages: the dot-matrix is generally faster, but the letters look "computerish"; they lack typewriter quality. Daisy wheel printers produce letters identical to those made by a typewriter, which is why daisy wheel printers are also called "letter-quality printers."

The dot-matrix printer forms characters in much the same way as your video display. That is, each letter is made up of a dot pattern. The actual print-head consists of a vertical column of pins (seven or nine, depending upon the brand of printer). Each pin is individually controlled by the computer, and any pin or pins may be extended to strike the ribbon and paper. As the print head moves across the page, it uses combinations of extended pins to form each character. It's something like those electric signs with moving letters formed by turning lightbulbs on and off.

Even with all of the movements required by the pin action, dot-matrix printers operate at from 120 to 160 characters per second in the ordinary print mode. When using the double-strike, or emphasized mode, which requires the pins to strike the same location more than once, the speed will obviously be reduced. Some dot-matrix printers are capable of printing type in several different sizes, and some use at least two different type styles ("regular" and italic). The cost of these printers ranges from $300—$2000. The higher-priced ones are faster, more rugged, and capable of more print varieties.

A daisy-wheel printer operates by pressing a pre-formed letter against the ribbon, just like a typewriter. The letters are on the ends of "spokes" radiating from the center of a wheel. Some printers operate with a "thimble," which has the letters arranged in a cup shape instead of a flat wheel. As we said, the advantage of letter quality printers is simply that they produce typewriter quality text. Their disadvantages are their cost (usually $1000 and up) and their slower print speed (45-55 characters per second). Some new daisy wheel models cost less than $1,000, but these have really slow print speeds. If you can live with 15 to 25 characters per second, look into these low-priced daisy-wheel models.

A third type of printer is beginning to appear — the non-impact ink-jet printer. The ink-jet printers are relatively new. While they are quieter than impact printers, they require a rough-coated paper to absorb ink and produce their darkest, most effective print. Three different technologies are used for these printers. One type uses a row of tiny, dot-matrix *holes*, instead of pins, and squirts tiny quantities of ink onto the paper in the dot-matrix pattern. The second type of non-impact printer is Apple's new Scribe model, which is a thermal printer. This type uses ordinary paper, but uses pins which transfer the dots to the paper by heating dot-shaped sections of a special ribbon. The third technology is the laser printer, which prints using laser beam technology. Laser printers are not yet available in a price range compatible with the //c as this is written. However, we would not be surprised to see an "insanely cheap" laser printer before 1986.

Plotters   A graphics plotter can be hooked up to your Apple //c. This device produces color charts by moving a pen on paper. The complexity of such charts is limited only your ingenuity and by the software that you buy or create to run the plotter. If you need to do much work that requires color displays such as slide presentations, graphs, or charts; consider the plotter. Again, make sure that your plotter operates through an RS-232 serial interface. Remember, the best way to avoid problems is to actually see the system set up by the dealer before you purchase one yourself.

By the way, in reminding you to make sure to have your dealer show you how the system components work together, we're not casting aspersions on dealers. The Apple folks have taken steps to improve overall dealer support, but that doesn't mean there won't be an employee out there who is having an off day. Insist on your right to make sure something works before you buy it. That's true for both hardware and software. By requesting this, you're being a wise consumer. You will in no way inconvenience a dealer who is concerned about his customers and wants you to be secure in your purchase.

Modems and Telephones   Once you have a printer and/or plotter up and running, you have more than half of the communications battle behind you. Sending and receiving data through a telephone is no more complicated than working with a printer or plotter.

To communicate with your computer by telephone, you hook a box called a "modem" (short for "MOdulator/DEModulator") to the other end of your RS-232 cable, and connect a telephone line to the modem. Modems are necessary because telephone circuits were designed for voice transmission, not high-speed data. The modem translates the flow of bits into sound signals and then back into bits. Since bits represent either "ON" or "OFF," there is one pitch or tone for on and another for off. The sound signals representing your data then go through the telephone wire as A. G. Bell intended. That two-note "song" is translated back into bits by the modem hooked to the receiving computer. Some software programs controlling the modems will verify the data during the transmission. Modems use the handshaking protocol method we described earlier to make sure that the receiver understands what was sent.

The //c is designed so that Serial Port 2 (the port with the telephone icon) is for modems. Modems come in two types: acoustic, and direct-connect. The acoustic modem is the one with a cradle that receives your telephone handset. You dial the number and place the handset in the modem. The tones go into the mouthpiece microphone, and are received by the earpiece. One disadvantage of acoustic couplers is that because any other sounds in the room with the telephone may also be transmitted, garbage may be recorded at the receiving end of your hookup.

Direct-connect modems plug into your phone line through wires, just like an extension telephone. Both 300 baud and 300/1200 baud modems are available from Apple and other manufacturers. In fact, the best hookup uses a Y-connector telephone plug adapter that allows you to connect a regular telephone and the modem into a modular telephone socket. Don't lift the telephone receiver while the modem is operating, or your transmission will be ruined.

Networks

The concept of computer networks is simple. Your computer is hooked up to other computers, data output, and storage devices via cables. For example, you and your colleagues in the same building can directly exchange information between computers, and all of you can share access to (and the cost of) a large, hard-disk data storage system.

While simple in concept, multi-user computer networks are anything but simple in their execution. First, like telephones and cable TV, they require that special wiring be installed in your building to connect the "networked" locations. (Note: this requirement may soon be eliminated by a system that uses signals superimposed on the existing AC electrical wiring in your building.)

Second, network systems require a control program to act as traffic cop for the inter-device signals. These signals allow one machine to interrupt another under defined conditions and priorities. For example, if Users B and E both want information from the storage disk at the same time, how are the requests handled? In order of request, or is E the boss and always given first call? If E is first, is B refused altogether, or told to wait? How long? Some networked devices accommodate more than one user by allocating time (splitting each second) and doing only a portion of each job at one time. This gives each user the illusion of immediate action. Other devices (such as printers) cannot do more than one job at a time.

Networking also involves passwords and other methods for data security. What information is to be accessed by User A only? What about information shared by Users A and C, but not by Users B, D, and E? All of these considerations enter into network design and selection. The variety of possibilities makes the design task considerably more complicated than it first appears to be.

A third complicating factor in networking is introduced when more than one type of computer is to be accommodated. A network containing only Apples with 6502 processors is easier to install than a network that includes Lisas, IBMs, 6502s, and data storage devices from still other manufacturers. Yet, by using the RS-232 serial protocols and your //c, it is possible to create such a network.

One likely approach to networking makes use of the //c's portability. The machine could be hooked into a network at its primary location, and then when necessary, unplugged and taken out on its own. Again, we say that there is no substitute in network design for an experienced dealer who can outline the problems and possibilities for you.

Information Utilities

An information utility is a service that allows your //c to be connected, through a modem, to a bank of mainframe computers that contain many kinds of information. You register as a customer, and each time you use the service your account is automatically charged for the time that you are connected to the system. You receive a monthly bill, similar to your telephone or electric bill, for services used.

The two best known general information services are The Source and CompuServe. Each has a telephone number in your locality, which you access via your phone and modem. With your //c connected directly to the utility's mainframe computers, the latest news, sports, and financial information are accessible. The services also provide access to specialized information collections or data bases. Two popular examples are aimed at frequent travellers: U. S. airline flight schedules, and information about restaurants in many cities. The most widely used specialized service is provided by Dow-Jones. It allows your computer to be hooked to this well-known news and financial wire service. With special software, you can receive the latest Dow-Jones ticker information and automatically update and evaluate your stock portfolio as often as you like. Other specialized data bases contain data useful for lawyers, physicians, other professions, and special interests.

Many people have predicted that we are only at the threshhold of an electronic information revolution. Your //c is designed to allow you to participate in this revolution via telecomputing.

Here are the contact telephone numbers for the four best known on-line data base services:

Dow Jones & Co
(800) 257-5114

The Source
(703) 734-7500

CompuServe
(800) 848-8199

MCI Mail
(800) 624-2255

9

Where To Find Help

Once you have become familiar with your //c, you will probably want to learn more about it — we have only scratched the surface of the capabilities of this remarkable little machine. Your Apple dealer remains a primary source of information about the //c and related products. Additional information is available from books (besides this one), magazines, and user groups.

Books   There are several kinds of computer-related books. Among the more common varieties are those that answer those who ask, "Why should I get a computer and what do I do with it after I get it?" You'll also find programming tutorials in several languages, machine-specific books, and software books that treat the general (how to use your word processor/data base/spreadsheet) and the specific ("*The Wonderfulness of* insert product name *here!*"). Since there were more than 900 book titles published in 1983 alone, you can see that you will have to be somewhat selective or your computer, your spouse or significant other, and possibly all other goods and chattels will be pushed out the door by your growing and groaning bookshelf.

Magazines   Computer-related magazines also fall into several categories: machine-specific, reader age-specific, software specific, and general interest. As with the books, you will have to look at some before deciding which ones have what you like. Here's an alphabetical list of Apple-specific magazines (the sharp-eyed reader will have determined the authors' bias by now):

A +
1 Park Avenue
New York, NY 10016
$24.97/yr, $43.97/2yr

Apple Orchard, the Premier Magazine for Apple Computer Users
P. O. Box 6502
Cupertino, CA 95015
$24.00/yr, $45.00/2yr

inCider, Green's Apple Magazine
P. O. Box 911
Farmingdale, NY 11737
$25.00/yr, $53.00/3 yr.

Nibble, the Reference for Apple Computing
P. O. Box 325
Lincoln, MA 01773
$26.95/yr.

Softalk
P. O. Box 7039
North Hollywood, CA 91605
$24.00/yr

General-interest magazines that contain information about Apple computers as well as many other brands include:

Creative Computing
P. O. Box 789
Morristown, NJ 07960
$24.97/yr.

Personal Computing
P. O. Box 2942
Boulder, CO 80322
$18.00/yr.

This new magazine is devoted to articles and programs of special interest to young people:

Digit
P. O. Box 29996
San Francisco, CA 94129
$12.00/yr (6 bi-monthly issues)

User Groups   A phenomenon of the Apple computer revolution has been the proliferation of Apple computer user groups in many cities around the world. Joining a user group will introduce you to other Apple users and provide the opportunity for you to learn more about your //c. There are a few exceptions, but most of the user groups welcome non-expert computer users and provide a place where unbiased experience can be shared. In such a group you are most likely to get the quickest answers to questions like, "How do I hook up a //c with the Frazzm X80 printer?" simply because someone else in the group has solved the problem and is willing to pass along the information to you.

User groups range in size from A.P.P.L.E., a large (20,000-plus) co-op buying and educational group headquartered in Kent, WA, to local user groups of 30-50 members. Some of the larger groups publish newsletters that extend beyond their "home" areas, and virtually all groups hold monthly general meetings. Many groups also conduct special-interest meetings on subjects ranging from programming to specific kinds of software (e.g. VisiCalc, or spreadsheets in general). Since these are mainly volunteer non-profit organizations not affiliated directly with Apple Computer, Inc., you will gain the most from membership by becoming an active volunteer. As your knowledge increases, you may enjoy the rewards of helping other members.

Some of the larger groups are listed below:

International Apple Core
908 George St.
Santa Clara, CA 95050
$30.00/yr (includes a subscription to *Apple Orchard* magazine)

A.P.P.L.E.
21246 68th Avenue South
Kent, WA 98032
$26.00/yr (plus $25.00 first-time fee; includes subscription to *Call-A.P.P.L.E.*)

San Francisco Apple Core
1515 Sloat Blvd., Suite 2
San Francisco, CA 94132
$20.00/yr (includes subscription to *The Cider Press*,
monthly newsletter)

Houston Area Apple Users Group
P. O. Box
Houston, TX 70
$20.00/yr (includes subscription to *The Apple
Barrel*, monthly newsletter)

Your odyssey with the Apple //c Mind Amplifier will
take you as far as you wish to go. Good luck and
Godspeed!

APPENDIX A - Binary, Decimal, Hexadecimal and ASCII

The following table shows the names of the symbols that are available from your //c keyboard, and their ASCII code values. It also provides a handy conversion chart between the three number systems used in conjunction with the //c. Note that decimal zero and decimal 128 are the same character. The character sequence shown between zero and decimal 127 repeats itself between decimal 128 and decimal 255, with the leftmost or "eighth bit" being set to 1 instead of zero.

The functions listed are those which are more or less standard. Many software programs employ other Control characters for specialized functions within each of those programs only.

Symbol or Key	(base 2) BINARY	(base 10) DECIMAL	(base 16) HEXADECIMAL	Function
Control - @	0	0	00	Null
Control - A	1	1	01	
Control - B	10	2	02	
Control - C	11	3	03	
Control - D	100	4	04	
Control - E	101	5	05	
Control - F	110	6	06	
Control - G	111	7	07	Bell
Control - H (or LEFT ARROW)	1000	8	08	Backspace
Control - I (or TAB)	1001	9	09	Tab
Control - J (or DOWN ARROW)	1010	10	0A	Linefeed
Control - K (or UP ARROW)	1011	11	0B	
Control - L	1100	12	0C	Formfeed
Control - M (or RETURN)	1101	13	0D	Carriage Return
Control - N	1110	14	0E	

Control - O	1111	15	0F	
Control - P	10000	16	10	
Control - Q	10001	17	11	
Control - R	10010	18	12	
Control - S	10011	19	13	
Control - T	10100	20	14	
Control - U	10101	21	15	
(or RIGHT ARROW)				
Control - V	10110	22	16	
Control - W	10111	23	17	
Control - X	11000	24	18	
Control - Y	11001	25	19	
Control - Z	11010	26	1A	
Control - [(or ESC)	11011	27	1B	Escape
Control - \	11100	28	1C	
Control -]	11101	29	1D	
Control - ^	11110	30	1E	
Control - __	11111	31	1F	
Space	100000	32	20	
!	100001	33	21	
"	100010	34	22	
#	100011	35	23	
$	100100	36	24	
%	100101	37	25	
&	100110	38	26	
'	100111	39	27	acute accent
(	101000	40	28	
)	101001	41	29	
*	101010	42	2A	
+	101011	43	2B	
,	101100	44	2C	
-	101101	45	2D	
/	101111	47	2F	
0	110000	48	30	
1	110001	49	31	
2	110010	50	32	
3	110011	51	33	
4	110100	52	34	

5	110101	53	35
6	110110	54	36
7	110111	55	37
8	111000	56	38
9	111001	57	39
:	111010	58	3A
;	111011	59	3B
<	111100	60	3C
=	111101	61	3D
>	111110	62	3E
?	111111	63	3F
@	1000000	64	40
A	1000001	65	41
B	1000010	66	42
C	1000011	67	43
D	1000100	68	44
E	1000101	69	45
F	1000110	70	46
G	1000111	71	47
H	1001000	72	48
I	1001001	73	49
J	1001010	74	4A
K	1001011	75	4B
L	1001100	76	4C
M	1001101	77	4D
N	1001110	78	4E
O	1001111	79	4F
P	1010000	80	50
Q	1010001	81	51
R	1010010	82	52
S	1010011	83	53
T	1010100	84	54
U	1010101	85	55
V	1010110	86	56
W	1010111	87	57
X	1011000	88	58
Y	1011001	89	59
Z	1011010	90	5A

[	1011011	91	5B	left bracket
\	1011100	92	5C	backslash
]	1011101	93	5D	right bracket
∧	1011110	94	5E	circumflex
―	1011111	95	5F	underline
`	1100000	96	60	grave accent
a	1100001	97	61	
b	1100010	98	62	
c	1100011	99	63	
d	1100100	100	64	
e	1100101	101	65	
f	1100110	102	66	
g	1100111	103	67	
h	1101000	104	68	
i	1101001	105	69	
j	1101010	106	6A	
k	1101011	107	6B	
l	1101100	108	6C	
m	1101101	109	6D	
n	1101110	110	6E	
o	1101111	111	6F	
p	1110000	112	70	
q	1110001	113	71	
r	1110010	114	72	
s	1110011	115	73	
t	1110100	116	74	
u	1110101	117	75	
v	1110110	118	76	
w	1110111	119	77	
x	1111000	120	78	
y	1111001	121	79	
z	1111010	122	7A	
{	1111011	123	7B	left brace
|	1111100	124	7C	vertical line
}	1111101	125	7D	right brace
~	1111110	126	7E	tilde
DELETE	1111111	127	7F	delete
Control - @	10000000	128	80	Null

APPENDIX B - Glossary

abort   to break off execution of a program. Accomplished on the //c by pressing CONTROL-C. Sometimes the break will occur immediately; sometimes you will need to press the RETURN key before the program will stop.

acronym   a name derived from the initials of the words used to describe it. In the computer world, the acronym often comes first and the words that it is said to represent are invented later, e.g., LISA.

algorithm   a step-by-step plan or list of procedures for solving a problem. With a computer, this process often involves repeating the same set of steps many times (iteration).

alphanumeric data   data consisting of combinations of letters and numbers or special characters.

analog computer   a computer designed to numerically evaluate physical data. Such data might consist of temperatures, solution concentrations, or pressure. Once the data is measured, it is changed into discrete numerical quantities.

Analytical Engine   the mechanical computing device, designed (1835) by Charles Babbage (1792-1871), but never actually constructed.

array   a table of items arranged in a row or rows. Allows easier manipulation of data.

ASCII   (pronounced like the device a donkey would use to unlock a door) American Standard Code for Information Interchange; the code used to designate each of the characters that can be understood by the Apple and other computers.

backup disk   the indispensible reserve copy of a disk program or data file, needed if the primary disk is damaged or lost. Always a nuisance until it's needed. Surveys show that the presence of a backup disk decreases the probability that the primary disk will be damaged or lost.

BASIC   Beginner's All-purpose Symbolic Instruction Code; the native higher-level language in the Apple //c, and another example of creative acronymania.

base   the number that supplies the basis for a numbering system. Our common decimal system uses the base 10 with the ten different digits 0, 1, 2, 3, 4, 5, 6, 7, 8, and 9; and "places" to indicate multiples of these values. For example, 17 means one 10 plus seven 1's.

baud rate   the number of bits going through a wire in one second, past a given point in the wire. The most common data transmission rates are 300, 1200, and 9600.

binary number system   a numbering system using base 2; there are two digits in the system, 1 and 0, used to indicate place values. Reading left to right, 1010 in binary reads $2^3 + 0 + 2^2 + 0$, or equals 10 in base 10.

bit   one binary digit, either a 1 or a 0, used to indicate an *on* or *off* electrical state within the computer.

block   in ProDOS, a predefined 512-byte section of the storage space on a disk. See also **sector**.

branch   the part of a program that directs the computer to depart from following a strict numerical sequence of program lines. The branch may be unconditional (always occurs at the same point in the program — uses the GOTO statement) or conditional (occurs only if a specified condition is met — uses the IF . . . THEN statement).

bug   an error in syntax or programming logic that causes the computer program to give the wrong results or cease to execute entirely. Name derives from a suicidal moth that fouled up the first computer and was blamed for subsequent problems as well.

byte   eight bits; in the 65C02 central processing unit these eight bits are required to designate any one character in the ASCII code. With eight bits, you can represent any number from 0 to 255.

CAD   Computer-Aided Design using computer graphics to aid in making drawings

CAI   Computer-Aided (or computer-assisted) Instruction.

cathode ray tube   a video screen.

central processing unit (CPU)   the main chip in a microcomputer; in the Apple //c it is a 65C02. Responsible for directing all the movement of data within the computer memory and for making all calculations.

character   one letter, number, punctuation mark or control symbol not displayed on the screen; also may include graphics symbols peculiar to a specific microcomputer or printer.

COBOL   COmmon Business-Oriented Language; the computer language most used on mainframe computers for business applications.

command   a word in BASIC or another programming language that tells the computer to do something.

computer   an electronic device capable of receiving, storing, processing, and giving out information or data.

concatenate   to link together; used in reference to string
                         manipulation. For example, if A$ = "John" and B$
                         = "Doe," you could concatenate the two into one
                         string variable with the statement C$ = A$ + B$.
                         PRINTing C$ would display "John Doe."

Control key   used on the Apple //c to allow non-standard control
                         characters to be created. Control characters are
                         primarily used to instruct the computer. For
                         example, CONTROL-S (pressing «CONTROL» and
                         «S» at the same time) stops scrolling on the screen;
                         pressing any key will cause the scrolling to con-
                         tinue. CONTROL-G makes the Apple //c beep;
                         CONTROL-J causes the cursor to drop one line on
                         the screen when you are using Applesoft.

cursor   the blinking box, underline, or checkerboard symbol
                         display on the screen to indicate where the next
                         character received from the keyboard will appear.
                         See also **prompt**.

daisy wheel printer the type of printer that will print letter-quality text.
                         A text character, molded on the spoke of a
                         printwheel, is printed when it strikes the printer
                         ribbon to produce an image on the paper in the
                         printer.

data   information; may be numeric, alphabetic, or a com-
                         bination of these.

data base   the entire amount of data pertinent to a particular
                         application; a collection of information.

**data base-management   a program designed to manipulate large amounts of
system**   data. Often included as one of the applications in an
                         integrated software program.

debug   the process of locating and eliminating errors in a
                         program. The primary source of frustration in
                         computer work.

decrement   to decrease the value of a variable, counter, or other value by a specified amount.

digit   a single numeral.

directory   the list or catalog of programs contained on a disk.

disk   also called floppy disk or hard disk; a magnetic circular object on which programs and data are stored for retention outside the computer.

disk drive   a machine that reads the magnetic information from a disk, and records new information on the disk.

DOS   disk operating system; the DOS controls the operation of the disk drive and access to other peripheral devices, and manages files. DOS is generally related to input/output of data.

documentation   the written information about a program or computer and how to use it.

dot-matrix printer   a printer that produces its characters on paper by having a column of pins hit the print ribbon in defined patterns. High-speed output without letter-quality characters.

edit   to rearrange, check, or change data to obtain a desired format; especially used in word processing.

ENIAC   the first electronic computer (1946). ENIAC is the acronym for Electronic Numeric Integrator And Calculator.

erase   to eliminate information from the video screen, the computer memory, or from a file.

external storage   media such as floppy disks used to store computer information where it will not be lost when the computer is turned off.

flowchart   a symbolic, graphic representation of the steps and sequence of a computer program. Drawing a flowchart before beginning to write program code helps to visualize the program to avoid logic errors.

format to prepare a disk to receive magnetic information. See **initialize**.

GIGO Garbage In, Garbage Out. The maxim of the computer industry.

graphics the display of pictures rather than letters and numbers on the video screen.

hard copy information printed out on paper, as contrasted with that stored on magnetic media.

hard disk a disk on which information can be stored much closer together on the hard disk than on a floppy disk. The hard disk is sealed in an air-tight container to protect it from contamination. Also called a Winchester disk.

hard sector refers to a disk on which the beginning of each track of information is marked by a physical hole in the disk. This hole is detected by the disk drive to correctly position the drive's read/write head. Apple disk drives use electronics to locate the beginning of a track rather than holes. See **index hole, soft sector**.

hardware all the machinery that makes the computer system run: computer, monitor, disk drives, printer, etc..

head the read/write mechanism of the disk drive. Similar in function to the head in your tape deck.

hexadecimal the base 16 number system. There are sixteen distinct digits; 0, 1, 2, 3, 4, 5, 6, 7, 8, 9, A, B, C, D, E, and F.

high-level language one in which the programmer can use familiar notation, such as English words. Assembly language uses mnemonics, three-letter codes that remind the programmer of their function; e.g., STX for STore in the X register, BNE for Branch if Not Equal, etc..

high resolution	a video display capable of showing many pixels or highly detailed graphics output.
I/O (Input/Output)	refers to the process whereby data is sent to and from the computer. Also used to describe the devices that perform both functions, such as keyboards, disk drives, etc.
index hole	the hole in a disk, detected by a photoelectric system. The hole indicates the start of a track or sector; not used on the Apple //c drives. See **hard-sector**.
ink-jet printer	one that does not strike the ribbon or paper, but rather shoots small drops of ink directly onto the paper through holes in the print head.
increment	to increase the value of a variable, counter, or other value by a specified amount.
initial value	the value assigned to a variable or array at the beginning of program execution. This process is called "setting the initial value," or "initialization." In Applesoft, the command RUN will automatically set all variables to zero (numeric) or null (alphanumeric).
initialize	to set initial values. Also to prepare a disk to receive data See **format**.
input	the process of getting information into the computer. Input is accomplished in many ways, including entering information via the keyboard, mouse, graphics tablet, or touch screen. Data may also be input via a modem, etc.. English language purists decry the use of a verb as a noun, as in the question, "Do you have any input?" See **output**.
integrated circuit	a circuit in which all the components are contained on a single chip of silicon. The chip is mounted in a clay slice. Pins along the side of the slice connect at one end to the circuit components and on the other

	end to the socket of a circuit board.
iteration	a one-time performance of an action or sequence of actions.
joystick	an input device used to move a cursor or other position-locator (in PacMan, for example). Used primarily for games and graphics programs. Named for the control stick in a small airplane.
justification	in word processing, indicates the alignment of margins, left, right, or both (full justified). Also used in spreadsheets to indicate the position of information within a cell. Also, the reason for purchasing the computer in the first place.
K	stands for kilo or one thousand; when referring to memory-size as in kilobytes, means 1000 bytes of information. A kilobyte is actually 2^{10} or 1024 bytes. The Apple //c has 128K of user-accessible RAM.
keyboard	the principal input device for entering alphanumeric data. Computer keyboards are similar to typewriter keyboards but include extra keys used in programming.
KISS	Keep It Simple Stupid. The prime command for programmers.
large scale integration (LSI)	construction of an integrated circuit chip that contains from 500 to 10000 individual circuits.
letter quality	printer output that appears similar to typewritten documents and is suitable for business correspondence.
light pen	a photosensitive input device; the screen position is detected by the CPU via light signals that have been turned into binary data and transmitted to the program. Useful in CAD, CAI and some drawing applications.
LIST	the BASIC command used to display program lines

on the screen, or on paper if your printer is active (turned on and the PR#1 command has been issued).

listing   the hard-copy version of a program or data.

logical operators   comparative operators used in calculations. These operations are represented by the following symbols:

Symbol	Name	Process
( )	Parentheses	grouping
*	Asterisk	multiply
/	Slash	divide
+	Plus	add
−	Minus	subtract

machine language   the lowest level programming language; the computer can process the information without intervening interpretation. Made possible because all instructions are in binary form.

mainframe computer   a large computer capable of handling millions of pieces of information at high speeds. Often used to control many remote terminals. Mainframes cost far more than the Apple //c.

memory   the portion of the computer where information is stored. See RAM and ROM.

menu   a screen display that lists user options in a menu format. Sample:

A. Run Space Vikings

B. Run SuperCalc

C. Run For It

Enter your selection.

microcomputer	any combination of hardware and peripherals built around a microprocessor. This type of computer was invented in the mid-1970's and is primarily intended for use by one individual.
minicomputer	a computer with intermediate (between micro- and mainframe) memory capacity and processing ability. Suitable for small to medium-sized businesses.
modem	abbreviation for MOdulator-DEModulator, a device to connect a computer to the telephone network for data transmission.
monitor	the video display screen. Also, the set of ROM routines in the computer that monitor internal operations such as memory management.
nanosecond	one billionth of a second; the time unit used in measuring the speed of the computer's internal operations.
nybble	four bits, or one-half byte.
number-crunching	using the computer to process extensive numerical data and/or complex mathematical formulas.
output	the delivery of information and/or calculations to a peripheral device such as a video screen, a printer, or a disk. See **input**.
parallel	the simultaneous transmission of several bits of data via parallel wires or cables. See **serial**.
Pascal	the structured, high-level language named for the French mathematician, Blaise Pascal.
patch	a hardware or software modification that changes the original operation of a piece of software to one more suited to the needs of a particular user. A program or code change that corrects a program error without having to completely rewrite the program.
peripheral equipment	all equipment attached to the computer, such as the

	monitor, external disk drives, the mouse, etc.
personal computer	a computer intended for use by one individual. See **microcomputer**.
pixel	picture element; refers to the smallest section of the screen that can be individually accessed from software; the smaller the pixel area, the greater the number of pixels and the higher the resolution.
plotter	an output device that draws hard copies of graphics information; often connected with analog computer devices. Also a soap opera character.
PRINT	the BASIC command to display information on the screen, the printer, or a disk.
printer	the principal peripheral for obtaining hard (paper) copy. See **Dot Matrix printer, Daisy Wheel printer**.
printout	a hard copy of a program listing or the output of data in a usable format such as that of an invoice, a check, a report, etc.
prompt	the symbol on the screen related to the particular language in operation.] is used for Applesoft, } for Integer BASIC, and * for machine language. The prompt appears at the left-hand edge of the screen to mark each new programming line; the cursor moves to indicate the next character position, but the prompt stays at the left.
protocol	the specific sequence of operations required to exchange information between computers or other communications devices; especially important in using modems.
random access	a file structure wherein any information element may be accessed directly. See **sequential access**.
Random Access Memory (RAM)	the portion of the computer memory that the user can modify. Since RAM memory is not permanent,

	anything stored in RAM is lost when the computer is shut off.
Read-Only Memory (ROM)	the portion of the computer containing built-in, unchangeable programs.
read/write head	the part of the disk drive that retrieves magnetic information from the disk, or places information on the disk.
recursive	refers to a computer procedure which calls itself; primarily used in Pascal and Logo.
REM	the BASIC command that lets you insert non-executed comments into a program listing. REM is short for remark.
reserved words	those words or phrases that are used as BASIC commands or statements and thus may not be used as variable names or parts of variable names.
robot	a computer-controlled device, used for repetitive tasks or for those that might be dangerous to a human operator.
rollover	the ability of the computer to remember the sequence of keys pressed; especially important when the computer operator is a rapid typist.
RUN	the BASIC command that causes the computer to execute a program in memory.
search	a data-base program function that selects records containing a specified sequence of characters.
sector	in DOS 3.3, a predefined 256-byte section of the storage space on a disk. See also **block**.
semiconductor	a material with electrical properties that fall between those of a conductor and an insulator; usually made of silicon, sometimes germanium.
sequential access	a file structure that stores information items one-after-another.

silicon	chemical element from which computer circuit chips are made.
simulation	a computer program that emulates a real-life situation such as real-estate management or ecological balance.
single sided	a disk that is certified by the manufacturer to store data reliably only on one of its sides.
soft sector	disk organization in which the start of information is indicated by a single index hole, or is controlled completely by the disk drive circuitry (the case with the Apple //c).
software	the programs that contain the instructions for computer operation. Software is found in many forms, including applications programs, simulations, games, systems programs, etc.
solid state	electronic system containing no moving parts or heated filaments.
sort	to arrange information in order, numerically or alphabetically.
spreadsheet	an electronic program that simulates the paper spreadsheet of an accountant. Spreadsheets are organized into rows and columns. Their design allows repeated recalculation of information repeatedly to test different "what-if?" hypotheses.
statement	a word in BASIC or other high-level languages. Used to give an instruction to the computer.
string	a group of characters (numbers, letters, or symbols).
syntax error	a message displayed on the screen to indicate that a typed command does not follow the accepted format of the program or the operating system being used.
systems analyst	a person who determines the best way to use the

computer for a particular situation.

TAB   the BASIC statement that moves the cursor a specified horizontal distance across the screen. Performs an action similar to that of the TAB key on typewriters.

terminal   an I/O device with a keyboard for input and a screen for output, connected to a mini- or mainframe computer. Some terminals use printers for output.

thimble   a form of printing element used on some letter-quality printers as an alternative to the daisy wheel.

track   one of a series of concentric areas of data storage on a disk; the disk used in the Apple //c has 35 tracks.

tractor feed   the means of controlling paper movement through a printer by pins fixed on wheels that mesh with holes along the edges of the paper.

UNIVAC   the first commerical computer (1951). UNIVAC is an acronym for UNIVersal Automatic Calculator.

update   to change information or data; to bring a system up to current standards or state-of-the-art.

user   you.

utilities   programs designed to help the programmer or end-user sort, copy, format, etc.

video screen   see CRT.

VisiCalc   the first spreadsheet program; use of this application program stimulated the sale of the personal computer.

voice synthesizer   a device that allows the computer speaker to emit sounds that resemble human speech.

Winchester disk see **hard disk**.

window an area on the screen. Technology which allows simultaneous access to several programs or applications in memory.

word processing using a computer to enter and manipulate text.

wraparound the ability of a word-processing program to keep words all in one piece by moving a whole word to the next line of text if that word will not fit intact within the defined margins of the previous line.

write protect to prevent information from being written to a disk; accomplished on Apple computers by using a special adhesive tab to cover the square slot in the side of the disk.

Index